HEALTHY COOKING
for
Singles & Doubles

Recipes for fitness for those who
eat alone or with one other person

By Eleanor Brown
and
Robin Detmer

FP

Fitness Publications, Ojai, CA

HEALTHY COOKING for Singles & Doubles is dedicated to all of the singles and doubles who want to eat well...simply and easily.

Published by:
Fitness Publications
306 E. Aliso, G Ojai, CA 93023

Cover & Interior Art: Oatley Kidder
Graphic Design: Fred Kidder
Book Design: Robin Detmer

Printed in the United States of America
Library of Congress Cataloging-in-Publication Data
Brown, Eleanor
Cooking healthfully for singles or doubles
Recipes for fitness

Library of Congress Card Number: 00-110986

Includes index
ISBN 0-9618805-8-9

HEALTHY COOKING FOR SINGLES & DOUBLES

INTRODUCTION

One morning at The Oaks, a guest said to me, "Eleanor, do you realize that most of the people who come to The Oaks live alone? Why don't you write a cookbook for them?" I now realize that it is not just Oaks guests who live alone, but many people in many stages of life.

This book is for all of you who live alone, or with just one other person. It is for college students, busy single professionals, newly weds, empty nesters and widows alike. Having granddaughters who are in college, I know that some of you live in groups, but do your own cooking. Some of you share meals with just one other person. Some of you live and eat primarily alone. Sadly, many people live on "fast food" and TV dinners because it seems like too much trouble to cook for one. This book will show you how easy it is to cook for one or two, and how much better your food will taste.

I have invited my granddaughter, Robin Dotson, to join me in this endeavor. She recently graduated from the University of California at San Diego. In college she primarily cooked alone or with a roommate and utilized quick and easy recipes. Since Robin is in her early 20's and I am in my mid 70's, we hope to present recipes that will appeal to our age groups and those in between. We are presenting only recipes that are very easy and quick to prepare, and that build health.

Most of the recipes in this book serve one or two. When the recipe is written for two, we include suggestions for using the second serving for those of you who are dining alone. There are a few recipes that serve more than two, and these are meant to create leftovers for nights when you don't want to or don't have time to cook.

Each recipe has been tested in our kitchen and simplified as much as possible. We hope that you find this book user-friendly and that you enjoy these recipes as much as we do.

If weight loss is your goal, remember that *diets don't work,* lifestyle changes do. A simple yet effective lifestyle change is: *eat less - move more*. This was written 2001; now we jump to 2005!

Please read the last page of this book called Notes from 2005 for an update on the authors. Robin has been promoted to co-author! You will also find current nutritional recommendations.

<u>Acknowledgments</u>

My heartfelt thanks to:

Granddaughter, Robin Dotson, without whom this book never would have been completed. She has been the perfect assistant... testing, tasting and writing recipes, as well as expertly doing all of the computer work.

Husband, Stan Brown, who tasted and critiqued our successes *and* our failures and did valuable editing.

Sheila Cluff who always encourages me in each new endeavor.

Dr. Ami Oren for some great recipes, as well as his endorsement of this book.

Mary Tabacchi, Ph.D. for encouragement, good recipes and her kind words on the back of this book.

And thanks to everyone else who donated recipe ideas!

Eleanor A. Brown

ABOUT THESE RECIPES

<u>EMBEDDED RECIPES:</u> These are simple little recipe ideas inserted into a recipe. They are shown in the index in *italics* with the page number. You will find the embedded recipe in CAPS under NOTES on the page listed.

<u>VEGETARIAN RECIPES:</u> There are many good vegetarian recipes in this book, but you can create even more by simply removing the chicken, tuna or meat. For example Tuna Noodles Romanoff becomes Noodles Romanoff on page 59. Tofu can be successfully substituted for chicken or meat in many recipes.

<u>GARAM MASALA:</u> This is a milder, sweeter form of curry powder... available in Indian and specialty food stores. We make our own by grinding in a coffee grinder: 1 T. cardamon seeds, 1 bay leaf, 1 inch stick of cinnamon and 1 tsp. each of cumin seeds, cloves, black peppercorns and coriander seeds.

<u>PASTA:</u> We used to dislike preparing pasta dishes because of the necessity of the extra step of boiling it in a separate pot. There are two recipes in this book that include cooking and serving pasta in the same pan as the rest of the ingredients. We have also learned to cook more pasta than I need and either freeze it with sauce or toss it with Italian dressing to add to green salads.

<u>SLOW COOKER:</u> The terms Slow Cooker and Crock Pot are interchangeable and we use both in this book.

HAPPY, HEALTHY AND QUICK COOKING!!!!

Equipping Your Kitchen

The following is a list of equipment that we would hate to be without:

- **Food Processor**: You will need this! It is possible to function without a blender if you have a food processor, and is worth having just to make Creamy Cheese.
- **Microwave Oven**: Essential for reheating leftovers and wonderful for poaching chicken breast and fish.
- **Crock Pot**: For slow cooking . . . it is so nice to come home to the aroma of a delicious dinner that is ready to eat.
- **Good Kitchen Scissors**: Excellent for removing all of the visible fat from chicken and miscellaneous meat . . . and for cutting raw meat into pieces.
- **Toaster Oven**: Saves energy and is wonderful for baking, toasting and broiling.
- **George Foreman Grill**: We have a small one that holds just two servings - very energy efficient. It grills quickly on both sides and drains off much of the fat from meat; it also produces wonderful grilled vegetables.
- **Individual Serving Dishes**: Soup mugs and augratin dishes work well, and go from your freezer to your microwave for "non-cooking" nights.

To freeze leftovers:
1. Place the food in the dish; for pasta with sauce, place the pasta on the bottom and top it with sauce.
2. Cover tightly with plastic wrap.
3. Place aluminum foil over the plastic wrap and freeze.
4. To reheat, remove foil and microwave.

TABLE OF CONTENTS

MARVELOUS MINI-MEALS, BREADS AND SANDWICHES:

SUPERIOR SOUPS:

SIMPLE SALADS & DELICIOUS DRESSINGS:

SUMPTUOUS SEAFOOD:

PLEASING POULTRY:

MISCELLANEOUS MEAT:

VIVACIOUS VEGETABLES: MAIN & SIDE DISHES:

DELICIOUS DESSERTS:

Marvelous Mini Meals, Best Breads and Super Spreads

It has been proven that people who divide their daily calories over three small meals and three mini meals control weight more easily than those who eat just three large meals. If you enjoy a healthy snack in between meals, you won't be as likely to get out-of-control hungry.

This chapter includes healthful sandwiches, a milk shake, a carrot bread and our all-time favorite, Creamy Cheese! Fruit and cottage cheese also makes a fine snack or mini-meal.

Just be sure to have that healthful snack before you get so hungry that you're buying a candy bar for a "quick pick up".

APPLE SLICES W/ ROASTED SOYBEAN BUTTER

A delicious and healthful snack anytime of day.
Servings: 1

1 apple, sliced and seeded
2 tablespoons soybean butter

1. Wash, dry, slice and seed the apple.

2. Spread soybean butter on each slice of apple and enjoy.

NOTE: Braeburn, Gala and Fugi are delicious. This is one of our favorite mini-meals. It will keep you going for a couple of hours. You can also stuff the soybean butter into celery for an even lower calorie snack or, of course, spread it on bread or crackers.

FOR CREAMY ORANGE ROASTED SOYBEAN BUTTER: Combine in the food processor: 1/2 C. nonfat cottage cheese, 1 T. orange juice concentrate & 1 T. Soybean Butter. This tastes wonderful and saves many calories!

Per Serving (excluding unknown items): 239 Calories; 11g Fat (38.7% calories from fat); 8g Protein; 30g Carbohydrate; 5g Dietary Fiber; 0mg Cholesterol; 157mg Sodium. Exchanges: 1 1/2 Fruit.

CARROT BREAD

A tasty breakfast bread that is great to have on hand.
Servings: 40

2 cups carrots, shredded
3 cups whole wheat flour
1 1/2 teaspoons low sodium baking powder
1 1/2 teaspoons baking soda
2 teaspoons cinnamon
1 teaspoon coriander
2 egg whites
1 egg
2 cups nonfat milk
1/4 cup honey
1 3/8 cups apple juice, frozen concentrate

1. Preheat oven to 350.

2. Combine dry ingredients and carrots in a large bowl.

3. Combine wet ingredients in a small bowl, and mix with the dry ingredients.

4. Divide between two nonstick sprayed loaf pans (8" x 4"), or make 4 small loaves (3" x 6").

5. Bake at 350 for 50 to 60 minutes. Turn bread out to cool on a rack.

SERVING IDEAS: Have it as a minimeal with lowfat cream cheese or as an accompaniment to breakfast, brunch or lunch.

NOTE: This freezes nicely.

Per Serving (excluding unknown items): 63 Calories; trace Fat (4.8% calories from fat); 2g Protein; 14g Carbohydrate; 1g Dietary Fiber; 5mg Cholesterol; 63mg Sodium. Exchanges: 1/2 Grain(Starch); 0 Lean Meat; 0 Vegetable; 0 Fruit; 0 Non-Fat Milk; 0 Fat; 0 Other Carbohydrates.

CHEDDAR CREAMY CHEESE

Our absolute favorite "calorie saver".
Servings: 38

4 ounces cheddar cheese, or your cheese of choice
2 cups nonfat cottage cheese

1. Place cheddar cheese in food processor and process.

2. Add cottage cheese and process until the mixture is smooth and creamy.

3. Place in a crock, press waxed paper on the cheese, cover and store in the refrigerator or freezer.

SERVING IDEAS: Toss with hot pasta, spread on whole grain nonfat crackers, use as a sauce on cooked vegetables or make a Frosted Pear by spreading the mixture on a cut pear half.

NOTE: This is a wonderful mixture to keep on hand to use as a spread, dip or sauce. We like to make a quart at a time, put it in three crocks and freeze two. When you use a stronger cheese you can save calories by using less of that and more of the cottage cheese.

Serving= 1 tablespoon

Per Serving (excluding unknown items): 19 Calories; 1g Fat (45.7% calories from fat); 2g Protein; trace Carbohydrate; 0g Dietary Fiber; 4mg Cholesterol; 50mg Sodium. Exchanges: 1/2 Lean Meat; 0 Fat.

EGGS SCRAMBLED IN MICROWAVE

A quick way to cook eggs that saves pan-washing.
Servings: 1

1 egg
1/2 teaspoon Butter Buds®
2 tablespoons nonfat cottage cheese
1 piece whole grain bread

1. Crack egg into a small bowl. Choose a bowl about the size of the bread.

2. Add cottage cheese and Butter Buds® and beat well with a fork, being sure to break the yolk.

3. Microwave, uncovered for 2 minutes until puffed. And at the same time toast the bread.

SERVING IDEAS: Serve in the cup in which the egg was cooked, along with whole grain toast....or turn the egg out on top of the toast.

NOTE: Eggs can be enjoyed for breakfast, lunch or as a minimeal. The cottage cheese replaces half of the egg with none of the fat and just as much volume.
 We sometimes, spread the bread with a bit of cholesterol reducing spread and enjoy with a glass of orange juice for a very satisfying breakfast.

Per Serving (excluding unknown items): 190 Calories; 6g Fat (28.4% from fat); 13g Protein; 22g Carbohydrate; 3g Dietary Fiber; 188mg Cholesterol; 387mg Sodium. Exchanges: 1 1/2 Grain (Starch); 1 1/2 Lean Meat; 1 Fat; 0 Other Carbohydrates.

GARDEN BURGER DELUXE

A tasty vegetarian favorite for lunch or dinner.
Servings: 1

1/4 pound meatless patty
1 hamburger bun, or 2 slices whole wheat bread
1 teaspoon ketchup
1 teaspoon mustard
1/4 tomato, sliced
1 lettuce leaf, washed and dried
1 slice onion, thinly sliced

1. Cook the meatless patty according to the instuctions on packaging. A toaster oven works well.

2. Lightly toast the hamburger bun or bread.

3. Spread ketchup and mustard on the bun.

4. Place the hot patty on the bun and top with lettuce, tomato and onion.

SERVING IDEAS: Enjoy a dill pickle or baby carrots on the side. You can top the burger with anything that you like, so be creative! Melt some cheese on the bread or bun and serve as an open faced sandwich.

NOTE: Our favorite meatless burger is Trader Joe's French Village Burger Champignon.

Per Serving (excluding unknown items): 403 Calories; 7g Fat (17.0% calories from fat); 17g Protein; 64g Carbohydrate; 13g Dietary Fiber; 18mg Cholesterol; 826mg Sodium. Exchanges: 1 1/2 Grain(Starch); 0 Lean Meat; 2 Vegetable; 1/2 Fat; 0 Other Carbohydrates.

OPEN FACE BAGEL SANDWICH

For all of us who love bagels.
Servings: 1

1/2 bagel, lightly toasted
1 ounce lowfat part-skim mozzarella cheese (one thin slice)
1 slice ripe tomato
1/4 ounce onion, minced (optional)

1. Lightly toast the bagel.

2. Top with cheese, tomato and onion. Broil for approximately 3 minutes until cheese is melted.

SERVING IDEAS: Do this with any bread you like. A slice of avocado on top is very good, as is a sprinkle of your favorite seasoning on the tomato.

NOTE: We like Trader Joe's French Yogurt cheese on this; it melts beautifully and is low in sodium and cholesterol.

Per Serving (excluding unknown items): 230 Calories; 6g Fat (23.2% calories from fat); 14g Protein; 31g Carbohydrate; 2g Dietary Fiber; 15mg Cholesterol; 398mg Sodium. Exchanges: 1 1/2 Grain(Starch); 1 Lean Meat; 1 Vegetable; 1/2 Fat.

PARMESAN TOAST

Crunchy parmesan topped toast to pick up a boring meal.
Servings: 2

1 whole grain English muffin, halved
1 teaspoon olive oil, or margarine
1 tablespoon grated nonfat parmesan

1. Split muffin.

2. Brush with olive oil and sprinkle with grated cheese.

3. Place under broiler and cook until brown and crusty.

SERVING IDEAS: This is a great addition to a soup or salad meal.

NOTE: This can be done with french bread or, better yet, whole grain french bread.

Per Serving (excluding unknown items): 87 Calories; 3g Fat (29.0% calories from fat); 3g Protein; 13g Carbohydrate; 2g Dietary Fiber; 0mg Cholesterol; 210mg Sodium. Exchanges: 1 Grain(Starch); 0 Lean Meat; 1/2 Fat.

PIZZA

An easy, healthful and delicious way to make individual pizzas!
Servings: 1

1 whole wheat English muffin, lightly toasted

2 tablespoons pizza sauce

1 cup vegetables (Our favorites include mushrooms, red bell pepper, chopped artichoke hearts, onion, and garlic), thinly sliced

1 teaspoon black olives, chopped

1 ounce lowfat mozzarella cheese, shredded or thinly sliced

1. Preheat oven to 400. (Toaster oven works very well.)

2. Cut the English muffin in half and lightly toast.

3. Top each half with sauce, cheese, olives, and vegetables. If you are using artichoke hearts, put these on last. Onion and garlic should also go towards the top.

4. Place the pizzas directly on the oven rack and bake for 10 minutes... or until cheese is melted.

NOTE: Top your pizza with whatever you like and have on hand. Be creative!
Another delicious combination is artichoke heart, fresh tomato and feta cheese. You do not need the mozzarella cheese if you use feta cheese. You can also make Pizza using mini whole wheat pita bread.

Per Serving (excluding unknown items): 238 Calories; 8g Fat (27.5% calories from fat); 14g Protein; 31g Carbohydrate; 4g Dietary Fiber; 15mg Cholesterol; 791mg Sodium. Exchanges: 1 1/2 Grain(Starch); 1 Lean Meat; 1/2 Vegetable; 0 Fruit; 1 Fat.

SALAD STUFFED PITA

A delicious veggie sandwich- perfect for summer days!
Servings: 1

1/2 pita bread
1 ounce lowfat cheddar cheese slice, jack cheese is good too
1/8 avocado, cut in thin slices
1 red onion slice (optional), cut thin
1 lettuce leaf, washed, dried and torn
1 tomato slice
2 cucumber slices
1 teaspoon vinaigrette, optional

1. Open the pocket of the pita bread half.

2. Stuff pita with a slice of cheese, avocado, onion, lettuce, tomato and cucumber.

3. Drizzle your favorite vinaigrette dressing on top of the vegetables.

SERVING IDEAS: Enjoy immediately with some cottage cheese or to complete a soup meal.

NOTE: You can use any vegetables you want to stuff the pita. Use left over salad makings, or even cooked vegetables for an easy lunch. In its simplest form, just stuff the pita with lettuce and tomato spread with a little lowfat mayonnaise.

Per Serving (excluding unknown items): 206 Calories; 9g Fat (38.3% calories from fat); 11g Protein; 22g Carbohydrate; 2g Dietary Fiber; 6mg Cholesterol; 340mg Sodium. Exchanges: 1 Grain(Starch); 1 Lean Meat; 1/2 Vegetable; 0 Fruit; 1 1/2 Fat.

SOY SHAKE

A smooth fruited soy drink.
Servings: 1

1/2 cup soy milk
1/2 cup canned pineapple chunks in juice
1/2 banana, frozen if possible

1. Combine all ingredients in a blender and process until smooth.

2. Pour into a glass for a mini meal.

SERVING IDEAS: Vary the fruit according to your mood and the season.
Fresh fruit works well!
If the banana is frozen, your drink will be thicker.
Peel and freeze bananas when they start to get too ripe so that you have
frozen banana on hand.
If you're out of soy milk, nonfat plain milk works and you can add powdered
milk for a thicker shake.

NOTE: This is an easy and delicious way to add more soy to your diet and
makes a wonderful mini-meal.

Per Serving (excluding unknown items): 170 Calories; 3g Fat (13.2% calories from fat); 4g Protein; 36g Carbohydrate; 4g Dietary Fiber; 0mg Cholesterol; 17mg Sodium. Exchanges: 1/2 Lean Meat; 2 Fruit; 0 Fat; 0 Other Carbohydrates.

ROASTED PEPPER & ARTICHOKE TAPENADE

An incredibly flavorful dip, spread or sauce.
Servings: 8

3 ounces marinated artichoke bottoms or hearts, drained
1/8 cup capers, drained
1/4 cup Parmesan cheese, freshly grated
1 tablespoon fresh lemon juice
1/4 cup fresh parsley, minced
2 cloves fresh garlic
3 1/2 ounces roasted red pepper, drained

1. Drop fresh parsley and garlic cloves into food processor while it is running.

2. Add remaining ingredients and process until quite smooth.

3. Store in a bowl and serve as a dip or spread with vegetables, crackers, rusks or toasted baguette slices.

NOTE: This is a special dip to serve to very special guests. They'll never be able to guess all of the ingredients, but are sure to enjoy it.

Per Serving (excluding unknown items): 27 Calories; 1g Fat (44.5% calories from fat); 2g Protein; 2g Carbohydrate; 1g Dietary Fiber; 2mg Cholesterol; 102mg Sodium. Exchanges: 0 Lean Meat; 1/2 Vegetable; 0 Fruit; 0 Fat; 0 Other Carbohydrates.

Superior Soups

Numerous tests have shown that those who have soup as a first course are less likely to over-eat than those who don't. Soup is comfort food: warm, filling and satisfying.

We like to make a meal of soup with salad and some whole grain crackers or, our favorite, Parmesan Toast. Sometimes we put the salad in a warmed Pita half for a simple meal which leaves only a soup mug and spoon to wash.

The recipes for main dish soups make enough to freeze portions for non-cooking meals. Freeze soup in mugs ready to go into the microwave for a quick meal. Keep a set of freezer-soup-mugs always filled and you'll never be forced to dine on fast food.

BROTH BREAK AT THE OAKS/ PALMS

A great way to use left over veggies; this is an amazingly satisfying pick-up for energy between meals.
Servings: 4

1/2 cup potato, red or white, diced
1 1/2 cups mixed vegetables (carrot, summer squash, celery, peas, broccoli, spinach, chard, etc.)
2 1/2 cups water

1. Combine and cook until veggies are tender.

2. Cool and puree in blender or food processor until very smooth. If there are lumps, strain the soup.

3. Reheat in a microwave or sauce pan, taste and add Jensen's broth powder or another salt substitute as needed.

SERVING IDEAS: Serve with whole grain crackers and creamy cheese as a mini-meal. Freeze in cups ready to microwave.

NOTE: We serve this midmorning at The Oaks and Palms and people always want the recipe. Use left over veggies for this...a good clean out the refrigerator recipe!

Per Serving (excluding unknown items): 48 Calories; trace Fat (4.6% calories from fat); 2g Protein; 10g Carbohydrate; 4g Dietary Fiber; 0mg Cholesterol; 211mg Sodium. Exchanges: 0 Grain(Starch); 1 1/2 Vegetable.

CHICKEN NOODLE VEGGIE SOUP

Chicken noodle soup with lots of veggies. A meal in a bowl...
and it starts with canned soup!
Servings: 2

2 cups fresh spinach, baby prewashed

1 cup fresh mushrooms, sliced 1" thick

1 cup broccoli flowerets, frozen

1 cup green beans, frozen

16 ounces can of lowfat chicken noodle soup, with wide noodles

2 tablespoons grated Parmesan cheese

1. In two pint sized soup mugs, place the spinach and then the rest of the vegetables.

2. If you have a half hour before you want to eat, leave the veggies covered so the frozen veggies can thaw, or cover and microwave for 3 minutes.

3. Add soup, dividing evenly between the cups.

4. Microwave about 3 minutes until hot.

5. Sprinkle a little grated parmesan cheese over the soup and enjoy with whole grain crackers.

NOTE: A wonderful dinner when you want a very light, very fast meal. Add a salad and/or sandwich if you're hungry.

Per Serving (excluding unknown items): 69 Calories; 2g Fat (22.5% calories from fat); 6g Protein; 9g Carbohydrate; 4g Dietary Fiber; 4mg Cholesterol; 130mg Sodium. Exchanges: 1/2 Lean Meat; 2 Vegetable; 0 Fat.

CHILLED AVOCADO SOUP

A chilled soup with an intriguing flavor...
Servings: 2

1/2 large avocado, ripe
3/4 cup nonfat chicken broth
1 tablespoon sherry , or orange juice concentrate

1. Slice avocado in half, leaving the pit. Store the half with the pit in a plastic bag in the refrigerator for a salad the next day.

2. Peel the other half and cut into 1/2 inch pieces.

3. Put the chicken broth, avocado and 1/2 cup water in a blender and process until very smooth and creamy.

4. Stir in the sherry (or orange juice).

5. Taste for seasoning and chill well.

SERVING IDEAS: Serve to your most sophisticated guest in chilled bowls, or eat it all yourself with a fruit salad. Save a slice of avocado to float on top or add a dollop of yogurt or sour cream..... nice but not necessary. Crunchy whole grain crackers are a must!

Per Serving (excluding unknown items): 87 Calories; 8g Fat (64.9% calories from fat); 5g Protein 4g Carbohydrate; 1g Dietary Fiber; 0mg Cholesterol; 192mg Sodium. Exchanges: 1/2 Lean Meat; 0 Fruit; 1 1/2 Fat.

CLAM CHOWDER WITH SOUR CREAM

This really good chowder reminds me of one that we used to spend hours preparing. This one is so easy and just as good!
Servings: 2

1 can clam chowder
2 small potatoes, peeled and chopped
1/2 cup lowfat sour cream
1/2 cup skim milk

1. Microwave potatoes in plastic covered soup mug for 3 minutes or until done.

2. Mix clam chowder, sour cream, and skim milk.

3. Add to potatoes in soup mug and microwave until hot.

SERVING IDEA: Add a can of clams and sprinkle with chopped scallions if you like...and a green salad is a must with some Parmesan toast.

Per Serving (excluding unknown items): 229 Calories; 4g Fat (16.6% calories from fat); 9g Protein; 38g Carbohydrate; 3g Dietary Fiber; 14mg Cholesterol; 396mg Sodium. Exchanges: 1 1/2 Grain(Starch); 0 Non-Fat Milk; 1/2 Fat; 1/2 Other Carbohydrates.

COSTA RICAN TOMATO SOUP

This has an unusual, but delicious flavor. A Spa guest favorite!
Servings: 2

1 1/2 cups tomato juice, unsalted
1/2 cup carrot, grated
2 tablespoons celery, minced
2 tablespoons chives, minced
3 tablespoons onion, minced
2 tablespoons green bell pepper, minced
1/8 teaspoon black pepper
1/4 teaspoon honey
2 tablespoons fresh parsley, minced
1/3 cup buttermilk

1. Place tomato juice in a sauce pan and bring to a simmer.

2. Add ingredients through honey to the tomato juice and simmer for 30 minutes until all vegetables are well cooked.

3. Add parsley and buttermilk to the soup and return to a simmer. Do not allow soup to boil after adding the milk.

4. Serve in heated bowls and garnish with a sprinkle of fresh parsley.

SERVING IDEA: Add a sandwich and you've got a great meal.

NOTE: If you like this as much as most people do, double the recipe and freeze some.

Per Serving (excluding unknown items): 76 Calories; 1g Fat (6.6% calories from fat); 4g Protein; 16g Carbohydrate; 4g Dietary Fiber; 1mg Cholesterol; 724mg Sodium. Exchanges: 0 Grain(Starch); 2 1/2 Vegetable; 0 Non-Fat Milk; 0 Fat; 0 Other Carbohydrates.

CUCUMBER SOUP

This is the best chilled soup we know!
Servings: 2

1 cucumber, hot house or english prefered
1 cup chicken broth
3/4 cup nonfat sour cream
1/4 cup buttermilk
1 tablespoon white wine vinegar
1 sliver garlic, minced
1/2 teaspoon salt
pinch white pepper

1. Wash cucumbers. English cucumbers don't need peeling, but regular cucumbers can be stripped every other inch or so.

2. Cut cucumbers into 1-inch chunks.

3. Puree all ingredients in electric blender or food processor. Add buttermilk slowly and be aware of consistency. It will thicken in the refrigerator so save any buttermilk not used in case you want to thin it later.

4. Refrigerate for 2-3 hours.

SERVING IDEAS: Serve in chilled bowls topped with any condiments such as hard-boiled egg, avocado, diced tomato, croutons or green onion.

NOTE: Everyone likes this! Serve as a special treat before a light meal. One of my oldest and dearest friends, Ginger Wilson brought me some of this after surgery.

You can make an excellent SOUR CREAM for this recipe by placing a scant 3/4 cup of nonfat cottage cheese in your food processor and adding lemon juice as you process the mixture. You will want a nice thick sour cream for this recipe; you can always thin the soup if needed, with a little more buttermilk.

Per Serving (excluding unknown items): 112 Calories; 1g Fat (8.6 calories from fat); 11g Protein; 17g Carbohydrate; 1g Dietary Fiber; 11mg Cholesterol; 1014mg Sodium. Exchanges: 1 Lean Meat; 1 Vegetable; 0 Non-Fat Milk; 0 Fat; 1 1/2 Other Carbohydrates.

MARY'S LENTIL SOUP

A simple, but satisfying soup.
Servings: 8

1 pound dried lentils
3 carrots, shredded or diced
1 clove garlic, minced

1. Rinse the lentils. Small lentils are preferred because they are more tender.

2. Cook lentils, carrots and garlic in a large stewpot with 2-3 quarts of water on medium heat for at least 2 hours.

3. Season with salt, pepper, curry and/or any other favorite seasoning to taste.

SERVING IDEAS: Serve lentils in warm soup bowls, garnished with sprigs of parsley or sauteed red pepper. Serve with Greek Salad in Pita Halves.

NOTE: Try adding a cup of barley to this recipe. It adds a pleasing texture. We like it with the addition of Curry Powder. This recipe from Mary Tabacchi personifies healthy eating. Freeze portions for non-cooking nights.

Per Serving (excluding unknown items): 204 Calories; 1g Fat (2.5% calories from fat); 16g Protein; 35g Carbohydrate; 18g Dietary Fiber; 0mg Cholesterol; 15mg Sodium.
Exchanges: 2 Grain(Starch); 1 1/2 Lean Meat; 1/2 Vegetable.

MUSHROOM BARLEY SOUP

Calling all mushroom lovers!
Servings: 4

1/2 cup barley, rinsed
2 ounces Crimini mushrooms
2 ounces Portobello mushrooms
2 ounces mushrooms (any kind)
3/4 cup diced onion
1/2 teaspoon dillweed
1 tablespoon garlic
1/2 teaspoon rosemary
1/2 cup white wine
1 teaspoon Butter Buds®
1 quart vegetable stock, or chicken stock

1. Combine all ingredients in a slow cooker and stir.

2. Cook on Low for 6 hours.

SERVING IDEAS: Serve hot with a salad. A spoonful of nonfat sour cream is a delicious addition. Serve Parmesan Toast or crackers for crunch.

NOTE: The longer this cooks the thicker it gets. If you like your barley firmer, opt for a shorter cooking time. Thin the soup as desired by adding more broth.

Per Serving (excluding unknown items): 288 Calories; 5g Fat (14.9% calories from fat); 10g Protein; 49g Carbohydrate; 8g Dietary Fiber; 2mg Cholesterol; 1650mg Sodium. Exchanges: 3 Grain(Starch); 1 Vegetable; 1 Fat; 0 Other Carbohydrates.

QUICK & EASY VEGETARIAN CHILI

The easiest vegetarian chili! Just open a few cans and simmer.
Servings: 4

28 ounces whole tomatoes, canned
16 ounces stewed tomatoes (Italian syle)
14 ounces kidney beans, canned
12 ounces Veggie Ground Round soy protein (YVES Veggie Cuisine)
1 tablespoon chili powder (or more for hotter chili)
1 tablespoon dehydrated onion flakes
1 tablespoon olive oil

1. Combine all ingredients in a crockpot.

2. Stir, cover and cook on Low for 4-6 hours until thick. This is the best way to bring out all of the flavors.

SERVING IDEA: Serve with sour cream or a dollop of Creamy Cheese. Delicious with a green salad and some tortilla chips.

NOTE: If you need this in a hurry do it on the stovetop. Simply combine all of the ingredients, bring to a boil, reduce heat and simmer on low for about 20 minutes.

Per Serving (excluding unknown items): 283 Calories; 5g Fat (14.5% calories from fat); 24g Protein; 39g Carbohydrate; 12g Dietary Fiber; 0mg Cholesterol; 827mg Sodium. Exchanges: 1 Grain(Starch); 1/2 Lean Meat; 3 Vegetable; 1/2 Fat.

QUICKEST MINESTRONE

A great way to use left over veggies and very good!
Servings: 6

3 cups soup stock (canned fat-free chicken broth works well)
3 cups marinara sauce (or Italian Sauce)
1 cup onion, chopped
1 large garlic clove, minced
1/4 teaspoon marjoram
1 teaspoon basil and oregano
2 ounces pasta
1 quart vegetables (zucchini, potato, carrot, bell pepper, eggplant, whatever you like), chopped
1 can kidney beans

1. Combine soup stock, marinara sauce, onion, garlic and herbs in a soup kettle and bring to a boil.

2. Add pasta and cut vegetables to soup and simmer until tender.

3. Add the cooked kidney beans and mix well. Taste and add seasoning as needed.

4. Serve in heated bowls sprinkled with Parmesan cheese.

SERVING IDEAS: Serve with salad and rolls for an easy and delicious meal.

NOTE: Make a large pot of soup and keep what you don't eat in the refrigerator or freezer for later. Take soup to work or school for a nutritious lunch or reheat for a night when you don't want to or don't have time to cook. This is a wonderful "clean out the refrigerator" dish.

Per Serving (excluding unknown items): 219 Calories; 3g Fat (12.2% calories from fat); 11g Protein; 38g Carbohydrate; 10g Dietary Fiber; 0mg Cholesterol; 524mg Sodium. Exchanges: 2 1/2 Grain(Starch); 1/2 Lean Meat; 1/2 Vegetable; 1/2 Fat.

VEGGIE BEAN SOUP ALA CHILANT

A splendid combination of beans, barley and many veggies.
Servings: 4

1 large onion, chopped
1/2 cup carrots, chopped
1/2 cup celery, chopped
1 cup frozen mixed vegetables (cabbage, cauliflower, broccoli or any other veggie you have on hand)
2 teaspoons olive oil
1 can diced tomatoes
1 cup 17 bean and barley soup mix (dry)

1. Chop up vegetables. Saute in olive oil until tender.

2. Add diced tomatoes and 17 bean and barley soup mix. Add water as needed to cover the beans.

3. Simmer for over an hour or two until beans are done.

SERVING IDEAS: Enjoy as is or combine with your favorite canned soup for a hearty meal. Serve with a salad and toast.

NOTE: Chilant Sprague, a favorite bridge buddy, makes a pot of this each week and uses it as a soup base with beef, chicken or tomato soup. We enjoy the flavor of the beans without additions. You choose! We also like to make the 17 bean and barley soup without sauteing the vegetables. Its very good with just some chopped onion and garlic; you get to taste the flavor of the beans! Left over ham is also a great addition to this soup. You are limited only by your imagination.

Per Serving (excluding unknown items): 203 Calories; 3g Fat (8.8% calories from fat); 15g Protein; 49g Carbohydrate; 24g Dietary Fiber; 0mg Cholesterol; 169mg Sodium. Exchanges: 2 1/2 Vegetable; 1/2 Fat.

Simple Salads & Delicious Dressings

Salads make a wonderful meal for one or two people. You can often build the salad right in the bowl for a quick and delicious entre with almost no clean up. (This is important to us!)

A few of these salads are side dishes, but most of them will serve as a meal.

Green leafy vegetables are a daily must in our lives, so we always have greens in the crisper ready to be used. We love the packaged baby greens, but like to mix them with Bibb or other green leaf lettuce.

There are many good dressings available now; but do try the Olive Oil & Balsamic Vinegar Sauce as well as the Walnut Oil with Dijon Mustard. Decalorize cream dressings such as Ranch or Blue Cheese by adding buttermilk. The more buttermilk you use, the lower the fat and calories. Plus, adding liquid thins the dressing and less clings to the delicious veggies.

ALBACORE WITH EGG SALAD

A delicious combination that takes care of one of your fish dinners for the week !
Servings: 2

6 ounces canned tuna in water (albacore is the best)
2 eggs, hard boiled
2 tablespoons lowfat mayonnaise
1 scallion, minced
2 cups leaf lettuce, washed and dried
2 medium tomatoes, cut in quarters

1. Combine the tuna, eggs, mayonnaise and scallion in a medium bowl. Try to plan ahead and chill this mixture for several hours after assembling the salad.

2. If you're dining alone, put half the mixture aside for another night or for a sandwich the next day. Cover it tightly!

3. Place a cup (or more) of greens on a plate. Put the albacore and egg mixture in the middle. Garnish with tomato pieces.

SERVING IDEA: Serve with whole grain crackers or bread. Try the Parmesan Toast in this book!

NOTE: Cooked artichokes or asparagus are wonderful with this salad! Avacado is sublime!

Per Serving (excluding unknown items): 239 Calories; 10g Fat (36.5% calories from fat); 29g Protein; 9g Carbohydrate; 2g Dietary Fiber; 218mg Cholesterol; 431mg Sodium. Exchanges: 4 Lean Meat; 1 1/2 Vegetable; 1 1/2 Fat; 0 Other Carbohydrates.

APPLE CHUTNEY

A sweet, sour and spicy blend of apples, dates and raisins.
Servings: 32

2 cups apple, diced small
1/4 cup dates, chopped
1/4 cup raisins
1/4 teaspoon coriander
1/4 teaspoon cumin
1/2 teaspoon garlic, minced
1/2 teaspoon fresh ginger, minced
1/4 cup apple cider vinegar
1/4 cup apple juice concentrate
1/4 cup water

1. Combine in a sauce pan and stir over low heat until liquid is absorbed and apples are tender.

2. Cover chutney and chill. This will keep for a long time in the refrigerator if you put it in a storage container and keep it covered.

SERVING IDEAS: Serve with curries, poultry and rice.

NOTE: If you like this as much as most people do, you might want to double the recipe. It adds a lot of flavor to many otherwise bland dishes.

Per Serving (excluding unknown items): 12 Calories; trace Fat (2.6% calories from fat); trace Protein; 3g Carbohydrate; trace Dietary Fiber; 0mg Cholesterol; trace Sodium. Exchanges: 0 Grain(Starch); 0 Lean Meat; 0 Vegetable; 0 Fruit; 0 Fat.

CARROT CASHEW SALAD WITH DATES

A delicious combination! A wonderful lunch in a bowl.
Servings: 1

2 cups carrots, grated
2 tablespoons cashews, broken (raw)
2 large dates, pitted & slivered

1. Mound the carrots in a bowl.

2. Circle the carrots with the date slivers.

3. Sprinkle the cashews over the top, grab a fork and enjoy a wonderful meal!

NOTE: This is even good without the dates, but don't add a lot of other stuff. The combination of the raw cashews with the carrots is amazing! You can grate the carrots by hand, use a salad shooter or do them in your food processor. I bought a salad shooter just so I could make this salad right in the bowl. Make it right before you want to eat it for the best results.

Per Serving (excluding unknown items): 250 Calories; 8g Fat (27.9% calories from fat); 6g Protein; 43g Carbohydrate; 10g Dietary Fiber; 0mg Cholesterol; 93mg Sodium.
Exchanges: 1/2 Grain(Starch); 0 Lean Meat; 5 Vegetable; 1 Fruit; 1 1/2 Fat.

CRAB SALAD

This is very good and very easy! Imitation crab with cottage cheese and mayonnaise.
Servings: 2

1 cup nonfat cottage cheese
1 cup imitation crab
4 tablespoons scallions, minced
2 tablespoons fresh parsley, minced
4 tablespoons lowfat mayonnaise
1 tablespoon lemon juice

1. Combine all ingredients and mix lightly.

2. Cover and refrigerate for at least an hour before serving. (You can actually serve it right away, but the flavors are better if they have a chance to blend together... and it's even better the next day!)

SERVING IDEAS: Scatter lettuce on a plate and put the crab salad in the center. Surround the crab mixture with wedges of tomato.

NICE ADDITIONS: Avocado, asparagus, artichoke hearts, hearts of palm... you get the idea.

NOTE: If you want more flavor, add a little mustard or grated Parmesan Cheese. We like it as is.

Per Serving (excluding unknown items): 278 Calories; 10g Fat (31.2% calories from fat); 29g Protein; 19g Carbohydrate; trace Dietary Fiber; 39mg Cholesterol; 1440mg Sodium. Exchanges: 4 Lean Meat; 0 Vegetable; 0 Fruit; 1 1/2 Fat; 1 Other Carbohydrates.

CURRIED ALBACORE W/ FRUIT & CHUTNEY

A salad furnishing a serving of fish, two fruits and a vegetable.
Servings: 2

1/4 cup nonfat mayonnaise
1 tablespoon orange juice, frozen concentrate
1 scallion, chopped fine
1 teaspoon curry powder, use half garam masala
1 cup grapes, halved
1 cup apple, diced small
6 ounces tuna in water, canned, albacore or pure white meat preferred
2 tablespoons walnuts, choped & toasted
2 cups baby lettuce leaves
2 tablespoons chutney (optional, but good)

1. Combine the first four ingredients for the dressing at least an hour ahead of time.

2. Combine grapes, diced apples and albacore right before serving. Toss with dressing.

3. Circle plate with baby greens, place a heaping cup of salad in the center and top with toasted walnuts.

SERVING IDEA: Serve one tablespoon of chutney on the side and garnish with fruit. Try the Apple Chutney recipe in this chapter or purchase the chutney.

NOTE: Even if the idea of mixing tuna with fruit sounds odd, please try this one if you like lightly curried food. This could also be done with chicken if you find yourself with some cooked chicken that needs to be used.

Per Serving (excluding unknown items): 351 Calories; 6g Fat (15.5% calories from fat); 30g Protein; 48g Carbohydrate; 8g Dietary Fiber; 26mg Cholesterol; 698mg Sodium. Exchanges: 0 Grain(Starch); 3 1/2 Lean Meat; 2 Vegetable; 2 Fruit; 1 Fat; 1/2 Other Carbohydrates.

GREEK SALAD IN PITA HALVES

A simple Greek salad slipped into a half pita.
Servings: 2

1 large ripe tomato, sliced 1/4" thick
2 large lettuce leaves, washed and dried
1 tablespoon feta cheese, crumbled
1/4 cup nonfat cottage cheese
4 Greek olives, cut in half and pitted
1/2 tablespoon fresh oregano, or to taste
2 marinated artichoke hearts, diced
1/2 tablespoon balsamic vinegar
1 pita breads, whole wheat fat free, halved and opened into pockets

1. Arrange tomato slices on lettuce leaves (one leaf per sandwich).

2. Sprinkle tomatoes with balsamic vinegar.

3. Combine cheeses, olives, oregano and artichoke hearts in a bowl and toss lightly.

4. Heat pitas.

5. Top tomatoes with cheese mixture (about 1/3 cup per sandwich) and slide into pitas right before serving. If you find it easier, add cheese mixture after sliding lettuce and tomato into the pita.

SERVING IDEAS: Marinated or grilled mushrooms, onions, peppers and grilled eggplant all work well as additions to this recipe. Feel free to add your own favorite Greek salad ingredients.

NOTE: Serve as a GREEK SALAD with extra lettuce, and add a little Pasta For Tossed Green Salads for a superb main dish salad.

Per Serving (excluding unknown items): 164 Calories; 5g Fat (27.5% calories from fat); 9g Protein; 22g Carbohydrate; 3g Dietary Fiber; 5mg Cholesterol; 345mg Sodium. Exchanges: 1 Grain(Starch); 1/2 Lean Meat; 1 Vegetable; 0 Fruit; 1 Fat.

GRILLED CHICKEN SALAD

A good main dish salad.
Servings: 2

2 boneless skinless chicken breast halves
1 tablespoon rice vinegar
8 ounces lettuce, prewashed
2 tablespoons honey mustard
2 tablespoons light soy sauce
1 teaspoon sesame oil
1 teaspoon fresh ginger
1 pinch black pepper, or to taste

1. Combine mustard, soy sauce, rice vinegar, sesame oil and fresh ginger to make marinade. Pour half marinade over chicken and reserve the rest for the salad dressing.

2. Let chicken marinade while heating the grill. Broil chicken for 10 minutes, turning once until cooked through and brown.

3. Cut chicken into strips. Serve over greens, topped with the reserved marinade. Season with pepper.

SERVING IDEAS: Garnish with orange slices. Serve with WON TON CRISPS (Bake won tons to crisp in the oven, painted with a little Soy Sauce).

NOTE: If you have time to marinate the chicken longer, the flavor will be improved. Make extra dressing and store some in the refrigerator for next time.

Per Serving (excluding unknown items): 196 Calories; 5g Fat (24.1% calories from fat); 31g Protein; 7g Carbohydrate; 2g Dietary Fiber; 68mg Cholesterol; 896mg Sodium. Exchanges: 0 Grain(Starch); 4 Lean Meat; 1 Vegetable; 1/2 Fat; 0 Other Carbohydrates.

HIGH FIBER SALAD

A meal in a bowl to build health.
Servings: 1

1 cup cabbage, coarsely chopped
1/2 large apple, chopped
1 large carrot, grated
1 orange, peeled, leaving as much white as possible.
2 tablespoons cashews, raw

1. Place cabbage in a wooden bowl. Top with apple and carrot.

2. Cut up orange over salad so juice is not lost.

3. Sprinkle salad with cashews and serve immediately.

NOTE: This high-fiber salad acts like a broom in your digestive tract. Chew it well and drink lots of water. A Monday of cleansing salads can often cancel out some over indulgence on the weekend.   This is always available at The Oaks/Palms for lunch or dinner.

Per Serving (excluding unknown items): 249 Calories; 9g Fat (28.4% calories from fat); 6g Protein; 43g Carbohydrate; 10g Dietary Fiber; 0mg Cholesterol; 44mg Sodium.
Exchanges: 1/2 Grain(Starch); 0 Lean Meat; 2 1/2 Vegetable; 1 1/2 Fruit; 1 1/2 Fat.

MEXICAN SALAD

This is a complete meal by itself...perfect for summer evenings.
Servings: 1

1 cup lettuce, washed and torn
1 tomato, diced
1 green onion, sliced
1/4 avocado, diced
1/4 cup kidney beans, drained
1 tablespoon salsa, medium or mild
1 teaspoon nonfat sour cream
1/2 ounce tortilla chips, broken

1. Put lettuce in a medium serving bowl. Top with tomato, onion, avocado, beans and cheese.

2. Mix salsa into sour cream. Toss salad with this mixture.

3. Top with crumbled tortilla chips and enjoy.

NOTE: This salad was created by my husband, Stan, and is a favorite of the whole family. You can vary the ingredients with great success, and only a bowl and a fork to wash! Look for lowfat, low sodium tortilla chips or make your own TORTILLA CHIPS by baking sliced corn tortillas in 350 oven until crisp...about 10 minutes.

Per Serving (excluding unknown items): 354 Calories; 12g Fat (29.7% calories from fat); 15g Protein; 51g Carbohydrate; 17g Dietary Fiber; 1mg Cholesterol; 183mg Sodium. Exchanges: 2 1/2 Grain(Starch); 1 Lean Meat; 2 Vegetable; 0 Fruit; 2 Fat; 0 Other Carbohydrates.

OJAI WINTER ORANGE SALAD

A delicious mixture of lettuce, orange, avocado and cashews.
Servings: 1

2 cups Bibb lettuce, washed and torn
1 medium orange, peeled and sliced
1 scallion, chopped
1/4 cup avocado, sliced
1 tablespoon cashews, toasted
2 tablespoons fat free honey mustard dressing

1. Combine lettuce, orange, onion and avocado.

2. Toss with dressing.

3. Top with toasted cashews.

SERVING IDEAS: Double the recipe and have a one dish meal, or serve as a side dish.

NOTE: We eat this salad in the winter when tomatoes are not very good. That's when Ojai oranges are at their best. There are many good fat free honey mustard dressings- find one you like! You can make this without the cashews or avocado to save on fat, but they add a lot.

Per Serving (excluding unknown items): 191 Calories; 10g Fat (42.7% calories from fat); 5g Protein; 25g Carbohydrate; 6g Dietary Fiber; 0mg Cholesterol; 49mg Sodium. Exchanges: 0 Grain(Starch); 0 Lean Meat; 1 Vegetable; 1 Fruit; 2 Fat; 0 Other Carbohydrates.

OLIVE OIL & BALSAMIC VINEGAR DIPPING SAUCE

This can be used as a dipping sauce or salad dressing.
Servings: 18

1/4 cup virgin olive oil
1/8 cup balsamic vinegar
1/4 teaspoon chili pepper flakes
1/2 teaspoon fresh garlic, mashed
1/8 teaspoon salt, optional
1/2 tablespoon parsley, minced
1/2 tablespoon fresh basil, chopped fine

1. Combine all ingredients and refrigerate for 4 hours. Store extra in a closed container in the refrigerator.

2. Serve as a dipping sauce for bread or veggies, or toss with a salad.

NOTE: This is much more heart healthy than butter and is delicious as a salad dressing.

Serving=1 tablespoon

Per Serving (excluding unknown items): 27 Calories; 3g Fat (97.8% calories from fat); trace Protein; trace Carbohydrate; trace Dietary Fiber; 0mg Cholesterol; 15mg Sodium. Exchanges: 0 Vegetable; 0 Fruit; 1/2 Fat.

ORIENTAL GREEN SALAD

A simple light accompaniment for Asian meals.
Servings: 1

1/2 cup iceberg lettuce
1/2 cup green leaf lettuce
1/4 cup carrot, shredded
1 tablespoon seasoned rice vinegar

1. Toss lettuce with vinegar.

2. Top with carrot shreds.

SERVING IDEAS: Serve immediately with any Asian or Indian meal.

NOTE: You can use plain unsweetened rice vinegar if you prefer and add a little honey. We like Nakano Seasoned Rice Vinegar with Roasted Garlic. Perfect for anyone who is trying to eat less fat. Thanks to Mary Tabacchi for this recipe!

Per Serving (excluding unknown items): 23 Calories; trace Fat (5.6% calories from fat); 1g Protein; 5g Carbohydrate; 2g Dietary Fiber; 0mg Cholesterol; 16mg Sodium. Exchanges: 1 Vegetable; 0 Other Carbohydrates.

PASTA FOR TOSSED GREEN SALADS

Adds texture and substance to your salads.
Servings: 6

1 1/2 cups cooked pasta, use twists or your favorite
3 tablespoons low calorie Italian salad dressing

1. Prepare pasta and rinse with cold water.

2. Mix with dressing, chill and toss with your favorite green salad.

SERVING IDEAS: Keep covered in your refrigerator and use with green salads, or just add cooked veggies for pasta primavera. Toss some of this with the Greek Salad instead of putting it in a pita half.

NOTE: This will keep covered for several days in your refrigerator.

Per Serving (excluding unknown items): 57 Calories; 1g Fat (15.4% calories from fat); 2g Protein; 10g Carbohydrate; trace Dietary Fiber; trace Cholesterol; 59mg Sodium. Exchanges: 1/2 Grain(Starch); 0 Fat; 0 Other Carbohydrates.

SPINACH WALNUT SALAD

A pleasing blend of spinach, walnuts & walnut oil spiced with mustard & balsamic vinegar.
Servings: 2

1 cup spinach leaves (stems removed), washed and patted dry
1/2 tablespoon walnut oil
1/2 teaspoon mustard, hot sweet is good
2 tablespoons balsamic vinegar
1 tablespoon walnuts, chopped & toasted

1. Mix oil, mustard and vinegar and whisk to mix well in salad bowl.

2. Add spinach and toss to coat leaves with dressing.

3. Top with walnuts and serve.

NOTE: You can save over 20 calories by leaving the walnuts out. Its very good without them, but they add a nice crunch. This is a great addition to any meal that needs something green. We also have served Spinach Salad dressed with just Walnut Oil and Sweet Hot Mustard. It, too, was very good.

Per Serving (excluding unknown items): 57 Calories; 6g Fat (83.4% calories from fat); 1g Protein; 2g Carbohydrate; trace Dietary Fiber; 0mg Cholesterol; 16mg Sodium. Exchanges: 0 Grain(Starch); 0 Lean Meat; 0 Fruit; 1 Fat; 0 Other Carbohydrates.

TOMATO, BASIL & MOZZARELLA SALAD

Good with a pasta dinner and french bread.
Servings: 2

1 large fresh tomato, sliced 1/4-inch thick
1 ounce mozzarella cheese (or French yogurt cheese), sliced thin and at room temperature
1 tablespoon fresh basil leaves, shredded
4 bibb lettuce leaves, washed and dried

1. Arrange lettuce on a chilled salad plate.

2. Top with tomato, cheese and basil.

SERVING IDEAS: This can be a first course or a side dish ... combined with a soup or pasta meal.

NOTE: If fresh basil is not available, use 1 teaspoon dried basil mixed with 1 tablespoon of chopped chives and/or parsley. Fresh mozzarella is best with this ... if you can find it. If not, make sure the cheese is at room temperature.

Do not attempt this unless you have some good vine ripened tomatoes!

Per Serving (excluding unknown items): 60 Calories; 4g Fat (53.3% calories from fat); 4g Protein; 4g Carbohydrate; 1g Dietary Fiber; 13mg Cholesterol; 65mg Sodium. Exchanges: 1/2 Lean Meat; 1/2 Vegetable; 1/2 Fat.

Sumptuous Seafood

Most of our scientific nutrition guidelines now list seafood twice a week as a must. This is mainly for the Omega-3 Fatty Acids present in fish. Salmon, tuna and trout are high in heart-healthy fatty acids.

This chapter includes recipes for baking, broiling, poaching, grilling and incorporating fish into mixtures to be microwaved. You will also find seafood in the soup and salad chapters. Feel free to make substitutions, for example you might use broiled swordfish instead of salmon.

BAKED COD FILETS

Crispy on the outside, moist and tender on the inside.
Servings: 2

1/2 pound cod fillets, fresh
1/4 cup lowfat 2% milk, to soak fish
1/2 cup fresh bread crumbs

1. Preheat oven to maximum temperature (~500).

2. Lightly spray a baking pan with nonstick spray.

3. Dip fish steaks in milk.

4. Coat fish with fresh bread crumbs. Try to cover the edges as well as the top and bottom.

5. Lightly spray bread crumbs with nonstick spray.

6. Place on pan and bake for 8 minutes.

SERVING IDEAS: Serve with a baked potato or yam and a steamed vegetable.

NOTE: Swordfish, tuna or any other favorite fish steaks would also be good for this. This recipe sounds wierd, but it works well. The crumbs turn brown and the fish stays very moist.
The best way to make BREAD CRUMBS is in the food processor:
Process a piece of fresh bread to produce fine bread crumbs.

Per Serving (excluding unknown items): 138 Calories; 2g Fat (11.9% calories from fat); 22g Protein; 7g Carbohydrate; trace Dietary Fiber; 51mg Cholesterol; 137mg Sodium. Exchanges: 1/2 Grain(Starch); 2 1/2 Lean Meat; 0 Non-Fat Milk; 0 Fat.

BAKED HALIBUT WITH MUSHROOMS & SOUR CREAM

This is our favorite way to cook Halibut...delicious!
Servings: 2

1/2 pound Halibut fillet (or whatever you choose)
2 teaspoons lowfat margerine
dash salt
dash pepper
dash paprika
2 teaspoons lowfat mayonnaise
4 teaspoons lowfat sour cream
6 fresh mushrooms, sliced

1. Preheat oven to 350.

2. Rub shallow baking dish with dab of margarine. Lay fish in dish, dab with margarine and lightly season.

3. Mix mayonnaise and sour cream in a small bowl. Cover fish with the mixture and top with mushrooms.

4. Bake at 350 for 30 minutes or until fish is flaky.

SERVING IDEAS: Serve with a baked potato and mixed steamed veggies.

NOTE: Be sure to use fresh Halibut. It is okay frozen, but much better fresh! Canned mushrooms are fine; we just prefer fresh.

Per Serving (excluding unknown items): 164 Calories; 5g Fat (26.2% calories from fat); 25g Protein; 4g Carbohydrate; 1g Dietary Fiber; 40mg Cholesterol; 98mg Sodium. Exchanges: 3 1/2 Lean Meat; 1/2 Vegetable; 1/2 Fat; 0 Other Carbohydrates.

BBQ TERIYAKI SALMON

Quickly BBQing (or broiling) marinated salmon makes it sweet and delicious.
Servings: 2

1/2 pound salmon steaks
1/4 cup teriyaki marinade

1. Place salmon in teriyaki marinade for at least 30 minutes. If you are using frozen steaks, thaw them before marinading.

2. Preheat the broiler or BBQ for about 10 minutes.

3. BBQ or broil for about 10 minutes on each side. Brush with teriyaki when you turn the fish for more flavor.

SERVING IDEAS: Serve with a baked potato and green salad.

NOTE: The fish should be flaky and done all the way through, but still moist. Keep checking it, so that it isn't overcooked. This recipe came from Robin's mother and my daughter, Kris Dotson. I have eaten it at her house many times and it is really good!

Per Serving (excluding unknown items): 172 Calories; 4g Fat (21.2% calories from fat); 23g Protein; 10g Carbohydrate; 0g Dietary Fiber; 59mg Cholesterol; 1256mg Sodium. Exchanges: 3 Lean Meat; 1/2 Other Carbohydrates.

BROILED SALMON WITH LEMON

An easy way to cook salmon with a buttery flavor!
Servings: 2

2 salmon steaks (4 oz.)
1 tablespoon lemon juice
1 tablespoon Butter Buds®

1. Sprinkle salmon with lemon juice and Butter Buds®.

2. Broil for 10-12 minutes.

SERVING IDEAS: Serve with a baked potato and steamed veggies or a salad.

NOTE: This started out to be more complicated with a sauce. However, the above was so good plain that we simplified it. If you want a sauce, mix lowfat mayonnaise with an equal amount of lemon juice.

Per Serving (excluding unknown items): 211 Calories; 6g Fat (26.0% calories from fat); 34g Protein; 4g Carbohydrate; trace Dietary Fiber; 88mg Cholesterol; 219mg Sodium. Exchanges: 5 Lean Meat; 0 Fruit; 0 Other Carbohydrates.

CRAB STUFFED POTATOES

A yummy crab mixture that blends beautifully with the potato.
Servings: 2

2 large baking potatoes, baked
4 ounces flaked, cooked crabmeat, canned
2 tablespoons plain nonfat yogurt
2 tablespoons lowfat mayonnaise
2 tablespoons chives, minced
2 teaspoons lemon juice
1 tablespoon chopped parsley
2 tablespoons Parmesan cheese, grated
pepper, to taste

1. Split the baked potatoes and press open.

2. In a small bowl, mix together the rest of the ingredients.

3. Spoon mixture into potatoes.

4. Broil about 4 inches below heat until golden (3-5 minutes).

SERVING IDEAS: Serve with the Spinach Salad in this book.

NOTE: Lucy Kelly Lucking served this as a most delicious hors d'oeuvre in tiny potatoes, but it makes a wonderful entree too! Imitation crab can be used as well as canned crab, however the canned flakes more easily.

Per Serving (excluding unknown items): 250 Calories; 6g Fat (20.7% calories from fat); 13g Protein; 37g Carbohydrate; 3g Dietary Fiber; 55mg Cholesterol; 597mg Sodium. Exchanges: 2 Grain(Starch); 1 Lean Meat; 0 Vegetable; 0 Fruit; 0 Non-Fat Milk; 1 Fat; 0 Other Carbohydrates.

POACHED SALMON IN WHITE WINE

Possibly the easiest and best way to cook salmon.
Servings: 1

4 ounces salmon steak
1 slice lemon
1/4 cup white wine

1. Preheat oven to 350.

2. Place salmon steak in a glass baking dish and top with a slice of lemon.

3. Pour the wine over the steak to cover, and cover baking dish with aluminum foil.

4. Bake 15 minutes at 350. The salmon should be opaque.
TO MICROWAVE: Cover with plastic wrap and cook on high for 8 to 10 minutes.

5. Cool and serve on a chilled plate lined with lettuce leaves.

SERVING IDEAS: Serve with the vegetables or fruit of your choice. This tastes especially good with fresh pineapple.

NOTE: You can also serve this hot with roasted potatoes and steamed veggies.

Per Serving (excluding unknown items): 183 Calories; 4g Fat (23.4% calories from fat); 23g Protein; 7g Carbohydrate; 1g Dietary Fiber; 59mg Cholesterol; 81mg Sodium. Exchanges: 3 Lean Meat; 1/2 Fruit.

TUNA-NOODLES ROMANOFF W/ MUSHROOMS

Marvelous blend of tuna, noodles & mushrooms in sour cream.
Servings: 2

7 ounces albacore, canned, in water
3 1/2 ounces wide noodles, cooked
1/2 can lowfat cream of mushroom soup
1/4 cup lowfat sour cream
1 cup sliced mushrooms, crimini preferred
2 tablespoons green onion, minced, use the whole onion

1. Boil a pot of water to cook the noodles, and preheat oven to 325.

2. While the noodles cook, blend together the sour cream with the soup.

3. Fold in the rest of the ingredients.

4. Put all ingredients in two individual lightly sprayed baking dishes.

5. Bake covered at 325 for 30 minutes OR microwave covered with plastic wrap for 4 minutes to heat.   For the microwave, punch a couple of holes in the plastic wrap. No need to spray the dish for microwave cooking.

SERVING IDEA: This cries for a crisp green salad.

NOTE: For NOODLES ROMANOFF, leave out the tuna. This is comfort food. These servings are generous and leftovers freeze well.

Per Serving (excluding unknown items): 372 Calories; 6g Fat (15.1% calories from fat); 36g Protein; 41g Carbohydrate; 2g Dietary Fiber; 94mg Cholesterol; 438mg Sodium. Exchanges: 2 1/2 Grain(Starch); 4 Lean Meat; 1/2 Vegetable; 1/2 Fat; 0 Other Carbohydrates.

TUNA SOUFFLE

Tuna in a strata ... very good and very easy!
Servings: 2

2 slices bread
2 ounces lowfat cheddar cheese, or other lowfat cheese
6 1/8 ounces canned tuna in water
2 eggs, beaten with fork until fluffy and yellow
1/2 cup milk
1 green onion, minced fine
dash salt and pepper
1 teaspoon dijon mustard

1. Spray the bottom and sides of a small baking dish with nonfat spray.

2. Toss the tuna, onion and bread together. Place in the bottom of the baking dish and top with cheese.

3. Combine eggs, milk and mustard. Pour over mixture in baking dish.

4. Set dish aside for 15 minutes or longer while you preheat the oven to 350. You can leave this refrigerated all day if you prefer... and bake it at your convenience.

5. Bake at 350 for 40 minutes until brown and puffed.

SERVING IDEAS: Serve with an Ojai Winter Orange Salad or a fruit salad.

Per Serving (excluding unknown items): 324 Calories; 10g Fat (29.0% calories from fat); 39g Protein; 17g Carbohydrate; 1g Dietary Fiber; 228mg Cholesterol; 719mg Sodium. Exchanges: 1 Grain(Starch); 5 Lean Meat; 0 Vegetable; 0 Non-Fat Milk; 1 Fat; 0 Other Carbohydrates.

TUNA SPINACH MELT

An easy way to get a serving of fish AND a green leafy vegetable. Quick and really good tasting!
Servings: 2

6 ounces tuna, choose white meat
1 pint fresh spinach, washed and stemed
6 ounces mushrooms, sliced 1/3" thick
1/4 cup onion, minced fine
2 ounces mozzarella cheese, part skim milk, sliced 1/8" thick

1. Place the spinach in two serving dishes.

2. Top with drained tuna.

3. Saute mushrooms and onion just enough to soften the onion OR microwave in a plastic bag for 1 minute.

4. Top spinach with 2 1/2 ounces mushroom mixture and an ounce of sliced cheese.

5. Cover tightly with plastic wrap and microwave for 2 minutes OR bake at 400 for 10 minutes, covered with aluminum foil.

SERVING IDEA: Serve with whole grain toast; this can become an open face sandwich or be eaten with a fork.

NOTE: If you can find Crimini mushrooms they have a wonderful texture. If you're making several of these, wilt the spinach first by covering and microwaving for 30 seconds. Repeat if needed.

Per Serving (excluding unknown items): 237 Calories; 9g Fat (36.0% calories from fat); 30g Protein; 7g Carbohydrate; 2g Dietary Fiber; 48mg Cholesterol; 210mg Sodium. Exchanges: 4 Lean Meat; 1 1/2 Vegetable; 1/2 Fat.

Pleasing Poultry

Chicken is such a natural in low calorie cooking that we had to restrain ourselves from using too many chicken dishes. But, you will find poultry in a fine variety of ethnic dishes as well as roasted, slow cooked, grilled, poached, stir fried and stewed.

You can substitute turkey for chicken and vice versa with good results. White meat is always preferred because it has less fat than dark meat. However, most of the fat and cholesterol is in the skin, so the most important thing in cooking poultry is to remove the skin.

Don't miss the recipe for Microwave Poached Chicken Breast. It produces moist and delicious chicken for salads and other recipes calling for cooked chicken.

ASIAN CHICKEN & VEGETABLE STIR FRY

A very good stir fry with a pleasing sauce.
Servings: 2

1 tablespoon cornstarch
3/4 cup lowfat chicken broth
1/2 tablespoon soy sauce
1/2 pound skinless boneless chicken breast, cut into strips
1 tablespoon fresh ginger, grated
1 teaspoon fresh garlic, minced
3 cups frozen stir-fry vegetables, or cut up fresh veggies
1/2 teaspoon sesame oil

1. Mix cornstarch with the broth and soy sauce until smooth. Set aside.

2. In nonstick skillet, stir-fry chicken until browned. Set chicken aside.

3. Add ginger and garlic and saute in sesame oil briefly. Add frozen vegetables, chicken and cornstarch mixture and stir. Cover and cook 5 minutes, or until veggies are tender-crisp. Do not overcook!

SERVING IDEAS: Serve immediately over couscous (very easy and fast to make!) or if you aren't a fan of couscous, you may prefer to serve the stir fry over brown rice or cellophane noodles (also very quick and easy). There will be additional calories for whatever you choose, but no additional fat. Add the Oriental Green Salad and you have a wonderful meal!

NOTE: Try substituting marinaded tofu for the chicken to make a delicious vegetarian meal! Just marinate the tofu in soy or teriyaki sauce and add after the veggies to heat through.

Per Serving (excluding unknown items): 223 Calories; 3g Fat (10.0% calories from fat); 35g Protein; 18g Carbohydrate; 4g Dietary Fiber; 66mg Cholesterol; 556mg Sodium. Exchanges: 0 Grain(Starch); 4 Lean Meat; 2 1/2 Vegetable; 0 Fat.

BOMBAY BREAST OF CHICKEN

Easy microwaved chicken breast, lightly curried.
Servings: 2

8 ounces boneless skinless chicken breast
2 tablespoons nonfat yogurt
2 teaspoons lemon juice
1 teaspoon soy sauce, low sodium
1/2 teaspoon curry powder
1/2 teaspoon Garam Masala, or mild curry

1. Place chicken in a baking dish.

2. Combine yogurt with the rest of the ingredients and mix with a whisk.

3. Brush each piece with sauce, covering well and let sit at room temperature for 30 minutes (or refrigerate for several hours).

4. Cover and microwave (high) for 3 minutes; turn and cook for 2 to 3 minutes until chicken is cooked.

5. Add additional sauce as chicken is served if you like.

SERVING IDEAS: This is very good with plain cooked basmati rice as it has a very nice flavor of its own. Quick cook some frozen or fresh oriental veggies to go with this and you have a light and luscious meal.

NOTE: The original version of this recipe came from Executive Chef David DelNegro of the Oaks.

Per Serving (excluding unknown items): 137 Calories; 2g Fat (10.3% calories from fat); 27g Protein; 2g Carbohydrate; trace Dietary Fiber; 66mg Cholesterol; 185mg Sodium. Exchanges: 0 Grain(Starch); 3 1/2 Lean Meat; 0 Vegetable; 0 Fruit; 0 Non-Fat Milk; 0 Fat.

BOW TIE PASTA CASSEROLE

A marvelous mixture of pasta, veggies, meat and cheese.
Servings: 2

1/2 pound lean ground turkey
1/2 medium onion, chopped
1/4 cup green pepper, chopped
1 cup mushrooms, halved
3 ounces pasta
1/2 cup lowfat cheddar cheese, grated
16 ounces canned tomatoes, broken up

1. Cook turkey, stirring to keep crumbly.

2. Add onion, pepper and mushrooms.

3. Arrange uncooked noodles over mixture and sprinkle with cheese.

4. Pour tomatoes over entire dish. DO NOT STIR!

5. Cover and bring to a boil. Reduce heat and simmer for 1 hour.

SERVING IDEAS: A sprinkle of grated Parmesan cheese is a nice touch. Serve with a spinach salad (Try the Spinach Walnut Salad in this book).

NOTE: Do this in a small skillet so the tomatoes completely cover the pasta. This mixture can be transferred to individual ramekins or bowls, covered with plastic and refrigerated to reheat for dinner. We love not having to cook the pasta separately. You could change the meat or make it meatless with more veggies. This freezes well and the servings are quite generous.

Per Serving (excluding unknown items): 436 Calories; 11g Fat (22.7% calories from fat); 39g Protein; 47g Carbohydrate; 5g Dietary Fiber; 79mg Cholesterol; 595mg Sodium. Exchanges: 2 Grain(Starch); 4 Lean Meat; 2 1/2 Vegetable.

CALIFORNIA CHICKEN CURRY

An old Spa favorite! Guests always want the recipe.
Servings: 2

1/2 pound boneless skinless chicken breast, cooked and cubed
1 teaspoon sesame oil, or canola
1 small clove garlic, minced
1/2 onion, minced
1 teaspoon curry powder
1/2 teaspoon fresh ginger, grated
1 pinch each: tumeric and allspice
1/2 cup tomato juice
1/2 cup green beans, cleaned
1/2 cup carrots, sliced
1 cup cauliflower, washed and cut
1/2 cup skim milk, or enough to cover vegetables
2 teaspoons arrowroot, dissolved in 2 T. hot water

1. In a small pot, cook onion and garlic in olive oil until tender.

2. Add spices, ginger and tomato juice and bring to a simmer over low heat.

3. Add vegetables and skim milk. Return to a simmer and cook about 30 minutes until vegetables are tender.

4. Stir in arrowroot mixture to thicken the gravy, and add chicken.

SERVING IDEAS: Serve hot with rice or cellophane noodles. Add Apple Chutney, raisins, toasted walnuts, cashews or chopped scallions.

NOTE: Use the fresh vegetables listed for best results. You can also make this a vegetarian dish by taking out the chicken.

Per Serving (excluding unknown items): 237 Calories; 4g Fat (15.8% calories from fat); 31g Protein; 19g Carbohydrate; 5g Dietary Fiber; 67mg Cholesterol; 355mg Sodium. Exchanges: 0 Grain(Starch); 3 1/2 Lean Meat; 2 1/2 Vegetable; 0 Non-Fat Milk; 1/2 Fat.

CANTONESE GRILLED TURKEY TENDERLOINS

Delicious marinated turkey breast (or chicken).
Servings: 2

1/2 pound turkey breast, boneless and skinless, cut in strips
1 tablespoon dry sherry
1 tablespoon soy sauce
1/4 tablespoon garlic, minced
2 teaspoons honey
2 teaspoons curry powder

1. Cut tenderloins in pieces and pound lightly with a mallet to even thickness.

2. Combine the rest of the ingredients and marinate for 5 minutes on each side.

3. Cook on grill over medium high heat to cook through.

SERVING IDEAS: This is wonderful with the Yellow Rice in this book. Add mushrooms and snow peas, microwaved or stir fried in a little soy sauce, for a splendid accompaniment.

NOTE: Large tenderloins may be cooked whole and sliced to serve, but be sure to pound down the thicker parts to ensure even cooking. This is also good with chicken breast, fish or meat.

Per Serving (excluding unknown items): 169 Calories; 1g Fat (6.0% calories from fat); 29g Protein; 8g Carbohydrate; 1g Dietary Fiber; 70mg Cholesterol; 572mg Sodium. Exchanges: 0 Grain(Starch); 3 1/2 Lean Meat; 0 Vegetable; 0 Fat; 1/2 Other Carbohydrates.

CHICKEN QUESADILLAS

This is a very good way to use up that left over chicken or turkey-with a taste of Mexico!
Servings: 1

2 corn tortilla
1/2 ounce green chiles, split in half
2 ounces cooked chicken, sliced
1/2 ounce cheddar cheese, lowfat, sliced or grated
1/2 ounce mozzarella cheese, part skim milk
1 teaspoon olive oil
1 tablespoon salsa

1. Oil the skillet and heat.

2. Place a tortilla in the skillet and layer chicken, chile and cheese on the tortilla.

3. Top with the second tortilla, cover and cook to brown the bottom tortilla.

4. Turn and cook until brown and crisp.

SERVING IDEAS: You can top your quesadilla with sour cream and salsa, or pick it up and eat it like a sandwich.

NOTE: If you have no chicken on hand, this is excellent with just cheese and green chiles- a Mexican grilled cheese sandwich. Try replacing the chicken with grilled veggies for a super healthful vegetarian meal. You can also use just one kind of cheese. Quesadillas are usually made with flour tortillas; we choose corn because its more nutritious and fat free.

Per Serving (excluding unknown items): 322 Calories; 12g Fat (32.9% calories from fat); 28g Protein; 26g Carbohydrate; 3g Dietary Fiber; 59mg Cholesterol; 357mg Sodium. Exchanges: 1 1/2 Grain(Starch); 3 1/2 Lean Meat; 1/2 Vegetable; 1 1/2 Fat.

CHICKEN SCALLOP WITH POTATOES

Tastes like a happy combination of scalloped potatoes and roast chicken with gravy!
Servings: 2

1 cup red potatoes, parboiled and sliced
1/2 pound boneless skinless chicken breast halves
1 teaspoon honey mustard
1/3 can lowfat cream of mushroom soup
1/3 cup nonfat yogurt

1. To parboil the potatoes in the microwave: Scrub the potatoes. Without drying them, place the potatoes in a plastic bag and microwave for 2 minutes on each side. Cool.

2. Preheat oven to 350.

3. Slice the potatoes and lay them in the bottom of a nonstick sprayed baking dish or two individual dishes.

4. Place chicken pieces on potatoes and brush with honey mustard.

5. Combine the mushroom soup and nonfat yogurt and pour over the chicken.

6. Bake uncovered at 350 for 35 minutes.

SERVING IDEAS: Sprinkle parsley, chives, Parmesan cheese or bread crumbs on top. Serve with a green salad.

NOTE: This recipe was included in one of the Pamphlets of Favorite Recipes that we did for The Oaks/Palms and it was so popular that we decided to include it in this book.

Per Serving (excluding unknown items): 208 Calories; 2g Fat (7.8% calories from fat); 30g Protein; 17g Carbohydrate; 1g Dietary Fiber; 67mg Cholesterol; 143mg Sodium. Exchanges: 1 Grain(Starch); 3 1/2 Lean Meat; 0 Non-Fat Milk; 0 Fat.

CHICKEN THIGHS W/ BARLEY, GARLIC & CHARDONNAY

Put it all in the crock pot in the morning and its ready to eat for dinner!
Servings: 2

1/2 pound chicken thighs without skin, boned
4 cloves garlic, sliced thin
1/2 cup barley, rinsed and drained
1 can fat-free chicken broth
1 1/2 cups chardonnay
1 teaspoon fresh rosemary leaves, snipped

1. Combine all ingredients in a slow cooker and cook on Low for at least 6 hours (3 1/2 hours on High).

2. Serve in bowls and top with chopped green onions.

SERVING IDEAS: The Spinach Walnut Salad is good with this.

NOTE: Don't miss this really easy and good dinner! These servings are very generous. We actually served four with this amount so if your appetite is small, freeze some. You can use any good white wine with this or substitute orange juice.

Per Serving (excluding unknown items): 378 Calories; 4g Fat (11.5% calories from fat); 24g Protein; 38g Carbohydrate; 7g Dietary Fiber; 54mg Cholesterol; 425mg Sodium.
Exchanges: 2 1/2 Grain(Starch); 2 1/2 Lean Meat; 1/2 Vegetable; 0 Fat.

CHICKEN WITH ARTICHOKE HEARTS

This, from our cover artist Oatley, is too good to miss!
Servings: 1

4 ounces boneless skinless chicken breast
1/2 cup canned artichoke hearts, cut in quarters
1/4 cup mushrooms, whole, Crimini preferred
1 tablespoon Parmesan cheese, grated

1. Place chicken in small baking dish and moisten with chicken broth, fruit juice or wine.

2. Cover with plastic wrap and microwave on high for 2 minutes. Turn and repeat.

3. Remove dish from microwave, cover chicken with artichoke hearts and mushrooms, sprinkle with Parmesan cheese and recover with plastic wrap.

4. Microwave 2 more minutes on high. (6 minutes total cooking time)

SERVING IDEAS: Serve with a crunchy green salad and whole grain bread.

NOTE: The artichoke hearts and chicken are absolutely delicious together. Add herbs if you like. If you use chicken tenders for this, cut the total cooking time to 5 minutes. We love the simplicity of this dish, as well as the low calories and ease of preparation. Oatley Kidder is not only a wonderful artist, she is a great cook!

Per Serving (excluding unknown items): 206 Calories; 3g Fat (14.2% calories from fat); 32g Protein; 10g Carbohydrate; 1g Dietary Fiber; 70mg Cholesterol; 465mg Sodium. Exchanges: 4 Lean Meat; 2 Vegetable; 0 Fat.

GRILLED GROUND TURKEY WITH MUSHROOMS

Good, easy and fast!
Servings: 1

1/4 pound ground turkey, formed into patty
3 ounces mushroom, sliced, crimini prefered
1 tablespoon low sodium soy sauce
1 clove garlic, crushed

1. Baste turkey patty with low sodium soy sauce and crushed garlic.

2. Place on hot grill with mushrooms and cover for 4 minutes. An electric skillet is good for this.

3. Uncover, turn patty and cook, stirring mushrooms until done.

4. Top each patty with mushrooms and serve hot.

SERVING IDEA: Serve with Parmesan Toast or a baked potato and lots of green salad.

NOTE: This is absolutely delicious as GRILLED GROUND SIRLOIN, however the fat content is significantly increased with sirloin. Look for very lean beef, or try half ground turkey and half ground sirloin for the flavor of beef with less fat. We like to do this in the electric skillet, but the George Foreman Grill will remove more fat.

Per Serving (excluding unknown items): 204 Calories; 10g Fat (43.0% calories from fat); 23g Protein; 6g Carbohydrate; 1g Dietary Fiber; 90mg Cholesterol; 710mg Sodium. Exchanges: 2 1/2 Lean Meat; 1 1/2 Vegetable; 0 Fat.

HEARTY TURKEY STEW

This is wonderful and very satisfying on a cold evening.
Servings: 2

1/2 pound turkey breast tenderloins
1 tablespoon olive oil
4 small potatoes, quartered
2 medium carrots, cut in 1/2" slices
1 large onion, chopped
2 cloves garlic, minced
8 ounces chicken broth
1/2 cup red wine
1/2 teaspoon thyme leaves
black pepper, to taste
4 ounces fresh mushrooms, cut in half

1. Cut up all vegetables on a large cutting board.

2. Heat oil in a pot over medium high heat. Place turkey, potatoes, carrots, onion and garlic in the pot. Cook and stir frequently until turkey is no longer pink- about 10 minutes.

3. Stir in chicken broth, wine, thyme and pepper. Bring to a boil.

4. Add mushrooms and stir. Turn heat to low, cover and simmer for about 40 minutes, or until veggies are tender.

SERVING IDEAS: Sprinkle snips of parsley over the top before serving. Serve with a dinner salad.

NOTE: Double the recipe and refrigerate or freeze individual portions for later. Always cover each individual dish with plastic wrap followed by tin foil to freeze. To reheat, take off the tin foil and microwave until hot. This recipe came from Nancy Krumpschmidt, my daughter Kris' best friend since kindergarten.

Per Serving (excluding unknown items): 383 Calories; 8g Fat (20.4% calories from fat); 10g Protein; 61g Carbohydrate; 8g Dietary Fiber; 0mg Cholesterol; 443mg Sodium. Exchanges: 3 Grain(Starch); 0 Lean Meat; 3 Vegetable; 1 1/2 Fat.

HERB ROASTED CHICKEN AND POTATOES

Chicken and potatoes roasted in a flavorful coating.
Servings: 2

3 tablespoons Dijon mustard
1 tablespoon olive oil
1 clove garlic, crushed
1 teaspoon Italian seasoning
2 chicken thighs without skin (all fat removed)
2 red potatoes, cut in wedges

1. Preheat oven to 425.

2. Mix mustard, olive oil, garlic and seasoning in a small bowl.

3. Place chicken and potatoes in a sprayed pan.

4. Using a basting brush or small rubber spatula, cover the chicken and potatoes with dressing.

5. Bake at 425 for 35 minutes or until potatoes are brown and chicken is done.

SERVING SUGGESTIONS: Serve with steamed veggies or a green salad.

NOTE: Use chicken breasts for this if you prefer.
Use this method to prepare ROASTED POTATOES without the chicken to serve with other dishes.

Per Serving (excluding unknown items): 222 Calories; 11g Fat (42.5% calories from fat); 16g Protein; 16g Carbohydrate; 2g Dietary Fiber; 57mg Cholesterol; 346mg Sodium. Exchanges: 1 Grain(Starch); 2 Lean Meat; 0 Vegetable; 1 1/2 Fat; 0 Other Carbohydrates.

HOT TURKEY SALAD

A delicious combination of turkey chunks and crisp celery topped with melted cheese.
Servings: 1

1/2 cup cooked turkey breast, cut in bite sized chunks
1/2 cup celery, chopped
1 tablespoon lowfat mayonnaise
1 scallion, chopped
1 ounce lowfat Swiss cheese, sliced thin or grated

1. Place turkey and celery in a small baking dish (round is best).

2. Mix in mayonnaise and the green part of the scallion so that turkey is lightly coated.

3. Top with the cheese, covering the mixture completely and cover with plastic wrap sprayed with nonstick spray.

4. Microwave on high for 2 minutes. Turn the dish and microwave 1 minute (or 30 seconds- to finish melting the cheese).

SERVING IDEAS: Serve with a green salad and whole grain toast.

NOTE: This is our favorite way to use leftover turkey breast. Be sure not to overcook. Round containers cook more evenly in the microwave. This can also be done in a regular oven; just cover and heat at 350 for about 20 minutes.

Per Serving (excluding unknown items): 231 Calories; 6g Fat (25.2% calories from fat); 37g Protein; 5g Carbohydrate; 1g Dietary Fiber; 93mg Cholesterol; 248mg Sodium. Exchanges: 5 Lean Meat; 1/2 Vegetable; 1 Fat; 0 Other Carbohydrates.

INDONESIAN CHICKEN

Spicy peanut sauce over chicken and rice. Delicious!
Servings: 2

1/3 Cup lowfat chicken broth
2 Tablespoons smooth peanut butter
1/2 teaspoon honey
1 teaspoon low sodium soy sauce
1/2 teaspoon red pepper flakes, crushed (use 1 tsp for spicier sauce)
1 tablespoon lemon juice
1 teaspoon sesame oil
2 boneless skinless chicken breast halves
2 green onions
1 cup cooked brown rice

Combine all ingredients through lemon juice in a container for the sauce. Mix well so peanut butter is blended in.

Cut chicken in bit-size chunks with a sharp knife or kitchen scissors. Trim any fat from chicken before cooking.

Heat sesame oil in a heavy skillet over medium high heat until hot. Add chicken and saute 2-3 minutes.

Turn heat down to medium and add the sauce and half of the green onions. Stir until chicken is well coated. Simmer until sauce is slightly thickened.

Remove from heat and serve over steaming rice. Garnish with the other half of green onions.

NOTE: This is good with the Ojai Winter Orange Salad or Ratatui in this book. If you prefer to buy peanut sauce, you can skip step one and the first six ingredients. Make extra sauce to save for later if you like.

Per Serving (excluding unknown items): 371 Calories; 13g Fat (30.5% calories from fat); 36g Protein; 30g Carbohydrate; 3g Dietary Fiber; 68mg Cholesterol; 342mg Sodium. Exchanges: 1 1/2 Grain (Starch); 4 1/2 Lean Meat; 1/2 Vegetable; 0 Fruit; 2 fat; 0 Other Carbohydrates.

LEMON CHICKEN

Tender breast of chicken in a lovely lemony sauce.
Servings: 2

2 boneless skinless chicken breast
1/2 can cream of chicken soup
2 tablespoons lemon juice
1/2 teaspoon dried herbs
pinch lemon pepper

1. Preheat oven to 400.

2. Spray two individual baking dishes with cooking spray. Place chicken in dish. Sprinkle with spices.

3. Combine soup and lemon juice. Pour over chicken. Refrigerate or freeze the rest of the soup for later.

4. Bake covered at 400 for 30 minutes. Remove foil, baste with juices and bake for 10 minutes more.

SERVING IDEAS: Serve with rice, fettucini or baked potato and salad or steamed vegetables.

NOTE: For a nice tang, put a little mustard on the chicken.

MICROWAVE POACHED CHICKEN BREAST

Moist, flavorful chicken to use in salads or recipes calling for cooked chicken.
Servings: 1

4 ounces boneless skinless chicken breast half
1 tablespoon chicken broth, or water

1. Place the chicken breast on a microwave-safe glass plate.

2. Drizzle with chicken broth.

3. Cover with microwave-safe plastic wrap and microwave on high for 3-4 minutes, turning chicken over after 2 minutes.

SERVING IDEAS: Use for any recipe that calls for cooked chicken breast. It's wonderful in sandwiches.

NOTE: If your chicken breast is frozen, add 3 minutes to total time and check by slicing through the middle. The chicken is done when no pinkness remains and the juices run clear.

Per Serving (excluding unknown items): 127 Calories; 1g Fat (11.2% calories from fat); 26g Protein; trace Carbohydrate; 0g Dietary Fiber; 66mg Cholesterol; 121mg Sodium. Exchanges: 3 1/2 Lean Meat.

TAMALES WITH MUSHROOM-CHILI SAUCE

A mild tamale dish- Mexican flavor without the heat.
Servings: 2

2 frozen tamales, thawed
1 can chicken chili
1 can lowfat cream of mushroom soup

1. Place tamales in individual baking dishes.

2. Mix chili and undiluted soup in a bowl.

3. Cover tamales with mixture and plastic wrap.

4. Microwave 3-4 minutes until hot.

SERVING IDEAS: Lowfat sour cream makes a good topping, and you'll want a green salad. Add a few tortilla chips for crunch.

NOTE: Tamales can be sliced and this could easily serve 3 people. Add a can of corn and it becomes four servings of TAMALE PIE. This is delicious! Use your favorite tamales and chili ... we like Trader Joe's Chicken & Cheese Tamales and Lowfat Chicken Chili. The mushroom soup makes a milder sauce; if you like more heat, leave it out.

Per Serving (excluding unknown items): 156 Calories; 8g Fat (46.0% calories from fat); 5g Protein; 16g Carbohydrate; 4g Dietary Fiber; 10mg Cholesterol; 744mg Sodium. Exchanges: 1 Grain(Starch); 1/2 Lean Meat; 1 1/2 Fat.

Miscellaneous Meat

All of my previous books have been Spa Cuisine from The Oaks and The Palms. Since we don't serve red meat at The Spas, it is not included in those books. However, most of the scientific nutrition community agrees that an occasional small serving of red meat is acceptable, so we have included a few of our lean favorites.

We occasionally enjoy a good steak, so have included the directions for grilling a really good, juicy steak. You'll also find a stir fry, some hot dog meals, a goulash, a pot roast and Doggie Bag Hash, a great way to use left overs.

Be judicious in your use of these dishes. Limit them to once or twice a week and keep the serving size to 3 or 4 ounces.

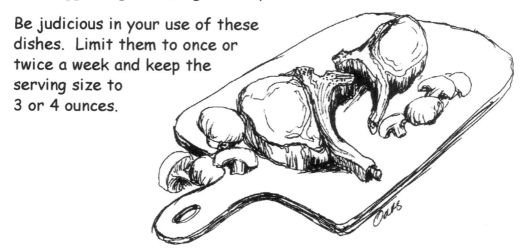

BOK CHOY AND BEEF

A good and quick "stir fry".
Servings: 2

1/2 pound sirloin steaks, trimmed, cut into 1/4" strips
1 clove garlic, minced
cooking spray
3 cups bok choy, sliced, white stems included
1/8 cup green onions, thinly sliced
1/2 cup diced tomato
1/8 cup nonfat beef broth
1 1/2 tablespoons low-sodium soy sauce
1 teaspoon arrowroot, or corn starch
1 dash pepper

1. Combine beef and garlic in a bowl. Chill 10 minutes.

2. Coat a skillet or wok with cooking spray and place over medium-high heat until hot. Add beef mixture and saute for 5 minutes, or until beef is done.

3. Remove beef from pan and keep warm.

4. Combine liquids with arrowroot and set aside.

5. Combine bok choy and green onions in skillet. Saute for 2 minutes.

6. Add beef and liquids. Simmer for 3 minutes until sauce is slightly thickened.

SERVING IDEAS: Serve with brown rice or cellophane noodles.
Garnish with tomatoes.

NOTE: This could also be done with chicken.

Per Serving (excluding unknown items): 270 Calories; 16g Fat (52.7% calories from fat);
24g Protein; 8g Carbohydrate; 2g Dietary Fiber; 71mg Cholesterol; 614mg Sodium.
Exchanges: 0 Grain(Starch); 3 Lean Meat; 1 1/2 Vegetable; 1 1/2 Fat.

DOGGIE BAG HASH

Leftover chicken, beef or lamb combines with fresh mushrooms and potatoes for a delicious main dish!
Servings: 2

2/3 cup fresh mushrooms, sliced
2 tablespoons onions, thinly sliced
1 teaspoon Canola oil, or margarine
1 cup potatoes, cooked and cubed
1/2 cup roasted skinless chicken leg meat, beef or lamb

1. Cook mushrooms and onions in oil in a large skillet over medium heat until tender.

2. Add potatoes and meat. Stir until heated through.

SERVING IDEAS: Serve with mixed steamed vegetables- they can be in the microwave while you heat and stir the hash.

NOTE: This recipe came from "doggie bagging" a lamb shank and making it into a wonderful meal for two. You can use any left over meat with good results. If you don't have cooked potatoes on hand, it is easy and fast to microwave them.

MICROWAVED POTATOES: Wash the potato, place in a plastic bag without drying the potato and microwave on high for 3 minutes on one side and 2 minutes on the other. This produces a "boiled" potato. For a baked potato, wash and dry the potato and microwave wrapped in a paper towel for 8 minutes.

Per Serving (excluding unknown items): 156 Calories; 5g Fat (31.0% calories from fat); 12g Protein; 15g Carbohydrate; 2g Dietary Fiber; 33mg Cholesterol; 38mg Sodium.
Exchanges: 1 Grain(Starch); 1 1/2 Lean Meat; 1/2 Vegetable; 1/2 Fat.

FRANKFURTER MEALS

For the times when you crave a hot dog!
Servings: 1

1 Healthy Choice Lowfat Frank, or your favorite brand

SERVING IDEA: Place frank in a plastic bag and microwave on high for 3 minutes or until hot and slightly puffed up. Serve hot dog on a toasted bun or folded piece of bread with ketchup, mustard and pickle relish. (193 calories; 5g fat)

SERVING IDEA: Cut up a hot dog in a half can of pork and beans. Cook over medium heat until steamy hot, or microwave for 3 minutes. This is an old childhood favorite. (204 calories; 4g fat)

SERVING IDEA: Place frank on 1/2 cup sauerkraut in a bowl, cover and microwave for 3 minutes until steamy hot.   This reminds us of bratwurst and kraut in Austria- wonderful!
NOTE: If you want to make the sauerkraut milder, grate some apple and stir it in before heating. (92 calories; 3g fat)

NOTE: Many of us want two frankfurters as a serving. If using the low fat variety, you can probably afford the calories. Hot Dogs are also good cooked on a George Foreman Grill.

Per Serving (excluding unknown items): 70 Calories; 3g Fat (31.9% calories from fat); 6g Protein; 6g Carbohydrate; 0g Dietary Fiber; 20mg Cholesterol; 440mg Sodium. Exchanges: .

HUNGARIAN GOULASH

Flavorful lean round steak in a sour cream tomato sauce!
Servings: 4

1 pound beef round steak, trimmed (all fat removed) cut in 1/2" cubes
1/2 cup chopped onion
1 clove garlic, minced
1 tablespoon flour
1/2 teaspoon salt
1/4 teaspoon pepper
1 teaspoon paprika
1/8 teaspoon dried thyme, crushed
1 bay leaf
7 ounces canned tomatoes
1/2 cup lowfat sour cream
1 tablespoon corn starch, whisked into sourcream

1. Put steak cubes, onion and garlic in a crock pot.

2. Stir in flour and mix to coat steak cubes.

3. Add all remaining ingredients, except sour cream.

4. Stir well, cover and cook on Low for 7-10 hours. Or cook on High 3-4 hours.

5. Thirty minutes before serving, add some of the gravy to the sour cream mixture, mix well and then stir back into the goulash.

SERVING IDEAS: Serve over rice or noodles. Cook the noodles right after you add the sour cream and rinse and hold them until the goulash is ready. I use bow tie noodles because they don't stick together.

NOTE: Put this in the crock pot in the morning, leave it on all day and come home to a heavenly aroma!

Per Serving (excluding unknown items): 240 Calories; 9g Fat (34.6% calories from fat); 29g Protein; 10g Carbohydrate; 1g Dietary Fiber; 78mg Cholesterol; 425mg Sodium. Exchanges: 0 Grain(Starch); 3 1/2 Lean Meat; 1/2 Vegetable; 1/2 Fat; 0 Other Carbohydrates.

JUICY GRILLED STEAK

Simple and good!
Servings: 1

1/4 pound top sirloin steak
1 teaspoon sesame oil
1 teaspoon soy sauce
1 teaspoon garlic, minced

1. Cut off all visible fat from the steak.

2. Combine oil, garlic and soy sauce. Cover steak with a thin coating of this mixture.

3. Cook on a preheated grill or barbeque on both sides until done to your taste. A George Foreman Grill works really well and fast for this.

SERVING IDEAS: Add salt and pepper after cooking to taste. Grilled onions or mushrooms are delicious on top! Serve with a baked potato and a green salad.

NOTE: The oil helps to keep the juices in the meat. Do not salt before cooking! Salt draws the juices out.
MICROWAVED MUSHROOMS: Slice them, add a dash of soy sauce, cover and microwave for 2 minutes while the steak is cooking. The same can be done for onions.

Per Serving (excluding unknown items): 188 Calories; 9g Fat (45.7% calories from fat); 23g Protein; 1g Carbohydrate; trace Dietary Fiber; 66mg Cholesterol; 406mg Sodium. Exchanges: 3 Lean Meat; 1/2 Vegetable; 1 Fat.

LUSCIOUS LAMB WITH POTATOES

Dr. Oren's wonderfully seasoned roasted lamb.
Servings: 2

2 lamb chops, lean (round bone)
1 tablespoon soy sauce
1 teaspoon lemon juice
1/2 teaspoon honey mustard
dash cayenne pepper, or to taste
1 1/2 tablespoons red wine
1/2 clove fresh garlic, crushed
1/2 teaspoon rosemary (or 2 tsp. fresh snipped)
2 small white rose potatoes, quartered

1. Marinade lamb in the rest of the ingredients (except potatoes) for an hour or longer.

2. Place chops in a small baking dish with the potatoes and the marinade.

3. Cover tightly with foil and bake at 150 for 2 hours or until done.

SERVING IDEAS: Serve with a mixed green salad and vinaigrette dressing.

NOTE: You need very good kitchen scissors to trim away all the fat before cooking. Round bone chops are leaner than most cuts, but there will still be visible fat to trim.

Per Serving (excluding unknown items): 261 Calories; 7g Fat (26.6% calories from fat); 28g Protein; 18g Carbohydrate; 2g Dietary Fiber; 79mg Cholesterol; 626mg Sodium.
Exchanges: 1 Grain(Starch); 3 1/2 Lean Meat; 0 Vegetable; 0 Fruit; 0 Fat.

MERLOT POT ROAST

A delicious and satisfying meal, especially on a winter evening.
Servings: 2

1/2 pound beef arm roast, fat removed
fresh ground pepper, to taste
2 carrots, rinsed and peeled
2 potatoes, rinsed and cubed
1/3 cup celery, chopped
1 onion, peeled and chopped
1 clove garlic, minced
1 pinch dried thyme
1 pinch black peppercorns
1 dried bay leaf
1/3 cup Merlot, or other dry wine
1 tablespoon tomato paste

1. Rinse beef, pat dry and sprinkle generously with fresh-ground pepper.

2. Cut carrots into sticks about 2 inches long and chop up the rest of the vegetables or us whole baby carrots.

3. In an electric slow cooker, combine carrots, onion, celery, potato, garlic, thyme, peppercorns and bay leaf.

4. Set beef on vegetables.

5. In a small bowl, combine wine and tomato paste. Pour over beef and vegetables.

6. Cover and cook until beef is very tender when pierced (about 5 hours on High or 8 hours on Low). If possible, turn meat over once during cooking.

SERVING IDEA: Serve with an Ojai Orange Salad.

Per Serving (excluding unknown items): 397 Calories; 18g Fat (40.8% calories from fat); 22g Protein; 37g Carbohydrate; 6g Dietary Fiber; 66mg Cholesterol; 174mg Sodium. Exchanges: 1 1/2 Grain(Starch); 2 1/2 Lean Meat; 3 Vegetable; 2 Fat.

Vivacious Vegetables-
Main and Side Dishes

Vegetables are, of course, one of God's greater gifts to us. They are packed with nutrients, fiber and flavor as well as being very low in calories.

Because they are so often overcooked, many people think they don't like vegetables. Stir frying, grilling, roasting and steaming in the microwave are wonderful ways to quickly cook most vegetables. They retain vivid color, firm texture and great flavor. Use these methods for side dishes. After many of our Spa guest's said how much they like their George Forman Grills, we purchased one. The first thing we cooked was grilled zucchini; it was delicious!

Beans, rice, pasta and corn tortillas with sauces help to bring substance to vegetarian main dishes. Beans are a very important source of fiber as well as protein, and you will find them used also in the soup chapter. Include beans several times per week in your menus. Most of these recipes freeze well, so stock the freezer with your favorites for non-cooking nights.

ANGEL HAIR PASTA PRIMAVERA

You can do this recipe all in one pot, and it is so good!
Servings: 2

14 ounces fat free canned chicken broth
1 teaspoon lemon juice, freshly squeezed
1 teaspoon lemon pepper, salt free
1/8 teaspoon saffron, optional
1/3 cup baby carrots, peeled
1/3 cup green beans, very young and thin, or frozen
1/3 cup broccoli florets
1/3 bunch scallions, cut in half inch pieces
2 plum tomatoes, cut in wedges
4 ounces angel hair pasta, broken in half
1 tablespoon romano cheese, grated

1. Place chicken broth and seasonings in a skillet and bring to a boil.

2. Add carrots, beans, broccoli and scallions. Stir, cover and cook 4 minutes.

3. Add tomatoes, cook one minute and remove veggies from broth.

4. Add pasta, stir, cover and cook 4 minutes, stirring from time to time. Check pasta for desired texture before removing from heat.

5. Toss pasta with veggies and serve topped with the romano cheese.

SERVING IDEAS: Add a green salad and some crunchy whole grain bread and dinner is served!

NOTE: Be sure to use the vegetables in the recipe. They work for color, texture and water content. We make this in our electric skillet.

Per Serving (excluding unknown items): 266 Calories; 2g Fat (7.9% calories from fat); 10g Protein; 52g Carbohydrate; 4g Dietary Fiber; 4mg Cholesterol; 240mg Sodium. Exchanges: 3 Grain(Starch); 0 Lean Meat; 1 1/2 Vegetable; 0 Fruit; 1/2 Fat.

CHILE RELLENO BAKE

An Oaks favorite- simple and delicious!
Servings: 2

4 ounces lowfat cheddar cheese, grated
4 green chiles, split in half
2 egg whites
1 egg
1/2 cup 1% low-fat milk
1/4 cup all-purpose flour
1/2 teaspoon cumin, ground

1. Preheat oven to 350. Spray two individual baking dishes with nonstick spray.

2. Layer chiles and cheese, ending with cheese

3. Combine eggs, milk, flour and cumin and pour mixture over chiles.

4. Bake at 350 for 40 minutes.

SERVING IDEAS: Serve with salsa, sour cream, and/or avocado slices. Add a fruit salad for brunch, lunch or dinner. Chips add a nice crunch.

NOTE: Daughter in law, Claire, cleans the seeds out of the chiles when she splits them. She made a casserole of this mixture for Christmas brunch and got raves. She does use full fat cheese and mixes jack cheese with the cheddar.

Per Serving (excluding unknown items): 268 Calories; 7g Fat (24.3% calories from fat); 26g Protein; 25g Carbohydrate; 2g Dietary Fiber; 108mg Cholesterol; 468mg Sodium.
Exchanges: 1 Grain(Starch); 3 Lean Meat; 1 1/2 Vegetable; 0 Non-Fat Milk; 1/2 Fat.

CREAMY POTATOES

A pleasing blend of cheese and sour cream with potatoes.
Servings: 2

2 medium potatoes, cooked and peeled
1/3 can lowfat cream of chicken soup
1/2 cup lowfat cheddar cheese, grated
1/3 cup lowfat sour cream

1. Preheat oven to 350. Slice potatoes and place in a baking dish.

2. Combine soup with cheese, reserving 2 T. of cheese. Cover and microwave to melt the cheese.

3. Stir in sour cream.

4. Pour over potatoes and top with remaining cheese.

5. Bake at 350 for 30 minutes or until heated through.

SERVING IDEA: Serve with a big veggie salad.

NOTE: This creamy dish is comfort food from Nancy Krumpschmidt ... her son's favorite. Crab or ham could be added to this. Vegetarians can substitute lowfat cream of mushroom or celery soup.

Per Serving (excluding unknown items): 193 Calories; 4g Fat (18.7% calories from fat); 12g Protein; 27g Carbohydrate; 2g Dietary Fiber; 14mg Cholesterol; 227mg Sodium. Exchanges: 1 1/2 Grain(Starch); 1 Lean Meat; 1/2 Fat; 1/2 Other Carbohydrates.

CURRIED VEGETABLE MEDLEY

A uniquely flavorful blend of vegetables- absolutely delicious!
Servings: 2

1 teaspoon olive oil
1/2 medium onion, chopped
1 clove garlic, minced
1/2 teaspoon curry powder (or more for stronger curry taste)
1/4 medium red bell pepper, chopped
16 fluid ounces stewed tomatoes (from can)
8 ounces garbanzo beans, canned, drained and rinsed
1/4 cup canned pineapple chunks
1 cup fresh spinach, thinly sliced

1. Heat the oil in a large nonstick skillet (electric skillet works very well).

2. Add the onion and garlic and saute for 1 to 2 minutes. Add the curry and saute another 30 seconds.

3. Mix in the pepper and cook for 3 minutes, or until softened. Stir in the garbanzo beans, tomatoes and pineapple.

4. Reduce heat to medium-low and simmer for 15 minutes. Stir in the spinach during the last 5 minutes of cooking.

SERVING IDEAS: Serve over cooked barley, whole wheat couscous, brown rice or as a side dish topped with toasted cashews.

NOTE: This sounds strange, but it is very good and definitely worth a try.

Per Serving (excluding unknown items): 267 Calories; 4g Fat (13.0% calories from fat); 9g Protein; 52g Carbohydrate; 9g Dietary Fiber; 0mg Cholesterol; 419mg Sodium. Exchanges: 1 1/2 Grain(Starch); 4 Vegetable; 1/2 Fruit; 1/2 Fat.

EGG FOO YUNG

A quick oriental pancake full of crunchy vegetables.
Servings: 2

1 egg
2 egg whites
1/4 teaspoon fresh ginger, grated
1/4 teaspoon garlic powder
1 green onion
2 tablespoons bell pepper, chopped
1/4 cup celery, chopped
1/4 cup mushrooms, chopped
1 cup mung bean sprouts

1. Combine egg, egg whites, ginger and garlic powder and beat lightly in a bowl.

2. Mix chopped veggies into egg mixture.

3. Heat a nonstick griddle and spray with nonstick spray.

4. Pour pancakes of the desired size. (Smaller cakes are easier to handle.)

5. Cook the pancakes until firm and then flip them over to brown the other side. The vegetables should remain crunchy.

SERVING IDEAS: Season with soy sauce. Serve with a veggie stir-fry or the Quick Hot Salad in this book. You can buy quite good Oriental Stir Fry mixtures.

NOTE: These are easy to make and very good. They do not reheat well, however, so it is best to prepare them right before serving.

Per Serving (excluding unknown items): 76 Calories; 2g Fat (26.9% calories from fat); 8g Protein; 6g Carbohydrate; 2g Dietary Fiber; 94mg Cholesterol; 101mg Sodium. Exchanges: 0 Grain(Starch); 1 Lean Meat; 1 Vegetable; 0 Fat.

ENCHILADA CASSEROLE

This is an enchilada-bean mixture. Easy and quite good!
Servings: 2

8 ounces tomato sauce
1 teaspoon dried onion
1/2 clove garlic, minced
1 1/2 teaspoons chili powder
1/2 teaspoon cumin
1/2 can pinto beans, drained
1/3 cup nonfat sour cream
1/3 cup nonfat cottage cheese
3 tablespoons lowfat cheddar cheese, grated
4 corn tortillas, torn

1. Preheat oven to 350.

2. Mix tomato sauce, spices and beans together. Mix sour cream and cheeses together.

3. In small casserole dish or individual baking dishes, layer tortillas, beans, and cheese mixture. Repeat until all ingredients are used, topping with the cheeses.

4. Bake at 350 covered for 20 minutes. Uncover and bake an additional 10 minutes.

SERVING IDEAS: Serve with baked tortilla chips and a green salad.

NOTE: This freezes well. Double the recipe and put the extra casseroles in the freezer for another night. Otherwise, save the extra 1/2 can of beans and sauce in storage containers in the freezer or fridge.

Per Serving (excluding unknown items): 387 Calories; 3g Fat (7.0% calories from fat); 25g Protein; 69g Carbohydrate; 17g Dietary Fiber; 8mg Cholesterol; 985mg Sodium. Exchanges: 3 1/2 Grain(Starch); 2 Lean Meat; 1 1/2 Vegetable; 1/2 Fat; 1/2 Other Carbohydrates.

FONDUE

A foolproof and delicious Fondue or Rarebit.
Servings: 2

1 can lowfat cream of celery soup, 10 1/2 ounces, undiluted
1/4 cup white wine, California Sauterne or other dinner wine
1/2 teaspoon mustard
1/2 teaspoon Worcestershire sauce
1 1/2 cups lowfat Swiss cheese, grated or cubed
1 egg, lightly beaten

1. In a saucepan blend together soup, wine, mustard and Worcestershire sauce.

2. Heat thoroughly. Add cheese, stirring over low heat until melted.

3. Slowly stir in lightly beaten egg and cook 2-3 minutes longer, stirring constantly over low heat until thickened.

SERVING IDEAS: Serve in a Fondue Pot with crusty French bread cut in cubes, along with blanched bite-sized broccoli crowns, cauliflower, asparagus and baby tomatoes. This may also be served over crisp toast as a Rarebit.

NOTE: This is sometimes our Christmas Eve supper.

MAGIC MACARONI AND CHEESE

A mostly nonfat mixture that tastes so creamy- it's magic!
Servings: 2

3 ounces macaroni, cooked, spiral
1 cup nonfat cottage cheese
1 ounce lowfat cheddar cheese

1. Preheat oven to 350.

2. Cook macaroni according to package directions. (We skip the salt and add Jensens Broth powder)

3. Combine cottage cheese and 1 teaspoon broth powder and mix into macaroni.

4. Divide mixture in two servings and place in two individual baking dishes. Sprinkle cheese over pasta, and bake, covered, at 350 for 45 minutes.

NOTE: For MAGIC MACARONI AND CHEESE PRIMAVERA: Steam two cups of your favorite vegetables (tender crisp or soft) and mix the vegetables into the pasta after step # 3. Zucchini, mushrooms, cauliflower, tiny slices of baby carrots, and chopped purple cabbage might be a good combination because of all the different colors. Please read the NUTRITIONAL NOTE below.

IMPORTANT NOTE: Do not try this in the microwave! It just doesn't work.

NUTRITIONAL NOTE: Current nutritional advice tells us to eat more vegetables. Adding all those vegetables adds less than 100 calories per serving, but the rewards are great. According to Dr. David Heber, Head of Nutritional Sciences at UCLA, the more different colors of fruits and vegetables we eat, the better our immune system will function.

Per Serving (excluding unknown items): 155 Calories; 1g Fat (7.5% calories from fat); 20g Protein; 15g Carbohydrate; 1g Dietary Fiber; 8mg Cholesterol; 387mg Sodium. Exchanges: 1 Grain (Starch); 2 1/2 Lean Meat.

PETITE PEAS IN SOUR CREAM

A delicious, creamy mixture with sweet little peas.
Servings: 1

1/2 cup frozen petite peas
1 teaspoon lowfat mayonnaise
2 teaspoons lowfat sour cream
dash garlic salt
pinch dill weed
1/2 lemon, juiced

1. Combine all ingredients in a small glass bowl and cover with plastic wrap.

2. Microwave 2 minutes.

SERVING IDEAS: Serve as a side dish with fish or chicken. Try stuffing a baked potato with the mixture, or serve over steamed vegetables.

Per Serving (excluding unknown items): 87 Calories; 2g Fat (20.3% calories from fat); 5g Protein; 14g Carbohydrate; 4g Dietary Fiber; 4mg Cholesterol; 116mg Sodium. Exchanges: 1/2 Grain(Starch); 0 Fruit; 1/2 Fat; 0 Other Carbohydrates.

QUICK HOT VEGGIE SALAD

This is actually faster than making a cold salad and very good.
Servings: 1

2 cups spinach leaves, washed
1 cup frozen broccoli flowerets
1/2 cup green beans, frozen
1/2 cup mushrooms, sliced 1/4" thick
1 tablespoon nonfat mayonnaise

1. Place spinach in a glass bowl and top with the other veggies.

2. Cover tightly with plastic wrap and microwave on High for 4 minutes.

3. Check to see if the vegetables are the way you like them. If they are too underdone, recover and microwave for another minute or two. (They will continue cooking for another minute after the microwave finishes so opt for underdone. You can always cook them more, but we don't know how to un-cook anything.)

4. Let the bowl sit for a minute, toss with mayonnaise and enjoy.

SERVING IDEAS: Pick up a roasted chicken to go with this, or poach some salmon or chicken breast.

NOTE: For a great tasting main dish, top the vegetables with a partially thawed serving of Frozen Eggplant Parmesan. Then cover and microwave until hot. We call this RON'S EGGPLANT DISH because my son in law, Ron Beall invented it.

Per Serving (excluding unknown items): 108 Calories; 1g Fat (7.3% calories from fat); 9g Protein; 21g Carbohydrate; 9g Dietary Fiber; 0mg Cholesterol; 272mg Sodium. Exchanges: 3 1/2 Vegetable; 0 Other Carbohydrates.

RATATUI

Vegetables stir fried in a mild curry create an addictive dish.
Servings: 2

1 cup eggplant, chopped
1 cup green and red pepper, chopped
2 cups tomato, chopped
1 cup onion, chopped
1 teaspoon garlic, minced
1 tablespoon virgin olive oil
1 teaspoon Garam Masala (or mild curry powder)
1 tablespoon balsamic vinegar

1. Heat oil in a wok or electric skillet.

2. Add cut veggies and seasonings. Stir fry until "mooshy".

3. Taste for seasonings and add as necessary.

SERVING IDEAS: Enjoy with steamed rice or as a veggie side dish.

NOTE: This recipe is from Dr. Ami Oren- it is loved by all of his four girls and we really like it too. Don't miss this one!

Per Serving (excluding unknown items): 162 Calories; 8g Fat (39.0% calories from fat); 4g Protein; 23g Carbohydrate; 6g Dietary Fiber; 0mg Cholesterol; 22mg Sodium. Exchanges: 4 Vegetable; 0 Fruit; 1 1/2 Fat.

SCOTT'S BEAN BOWL

Easy and good for lunch or dinner when you're in a hurry.
Servings: 1

1/3 cup canned pinto beans, drained
1 tablespoon chopped onion
1 ounce lowfat cheddar cheese, grated
1/2 tomato, diced
salsa, to taste
1 corn tortilla, heated

1. In a microwaveable bowl heat pinto beans for 2 minutes, or until hot.

2. Meanwhile, chop onions and tomato and grate cheese.

3. Top steaming beans with cheese, onion, tomato and salsa.

4. Serve with a hot corn tortilla on the side.

SERVING IDEAS: This is also good with black beans, or a mixture of black and pinto. Try adding lettuce, avocado and sour cream for a complete meal.

NOTE: This recipe came from Robin's boyfriend, Scott Detmer... created during his days as a student at UCSD. He buys dried pinto beans, cooks a pot of them and uses them in this recipe as well as burritos and tostadas. Follow the directions on the package to cook dried beans. They are inexpensive and can be the start of many delicious dishes.

Per Serving (excluding unknown items): 184 Calories; 3g Fat (14.7% calories from fat); 13g Protein; 28g Carbohydrate; 5g Dietary Fiber; 6mg Cholesterol; 552mg Sodium. Exchanges: 1 1/2 Grain(Starch); 1 Lean Meat; 1/2 Vegetable; 0 Fat.

SPINACH STUFFED PORTOBELO MUSHROOMS

A delicious mixture stuffed in giant mushrooms.
Servings: 2

4 Portobelo mushroom, stems removed and chopped
1 cup spinach, chopped
1 green onion, chopped
1/2 cup nonfat cottage cheese
1/4 cup lowfat cheddar cheese, grated
1/4 cup lowfat sour cream
1/4 teaspoon dill weed

1. Preheat oven to 350.

2. Prepare mushrooms and place in a baking dish.

3. Combine chopped veggies and the rest of the ingredients.

4. Stuff filling into mushrooms, pressing well into mushroom and mounding up.

5. Cover and bake at 350 for 15 minutes, or microwave 4 minutes.

SERVING IDEAS: Serve with a baked potato and a spinach salad.

NOTE: We had some filling left after stuffing the mushrooms, so we covered the bowl and microwaved for 2 minutes. We used this as a spread on crackers which was delicious! You can also just slice off the stem of a Portobelo mushroom and grill it with your favorite herbs for a wonderful PORTOBELO MUSHROOM STEAK.

Per Serving (excluding unknown items): 101 Calories; 2g Fat (22.1% calories from fat); 13g Protein; 7g Carbohydrate; 1g Dietary Fiber; 11mg Cholesterol; 284mg Sodium. Exchanges: 1 1/2 Lean Meat; 0 Vegetable; 1/2 Fat; 0 Other Carbohydrates.

STEAMED VEGGIES WITH MOZZARELLA

A cheesy mixture of cooked vegetables.
Servings: 1

1/3 cup carrots, scrubbed and cut in thin slices
1/3 cup broccoli, cut in 1" pieces
1/3 cup cauliflower flowerets
1/3 cup green beans, cut
1/3 cup celery, cut 1/2" thick
1/3 cup fresh mushrooms
2 ounces lowfat mozzarella cheese (or French yogurt cheese), grated

1. Place vegetables in a microwaveable bowl.

2. Cover with plastic wrap and microwave on high for 3-4 minutes.

3. Sprinkle cheese on vegetables while they are still very hot.

NOTE: You can use any kind of vegetables in this. Also try different types of cheese. Spinach or chard is wonderful topped with swiss cheese.

SERVING IDEA: Serve with whole grain crackers or toast. Add a baked potato for a satisfying meal.

Per Serving (excluding unknown items): 216 Calories; 10g Fat (40.8% calories from fat); 19g Protein; 14g Carbohydrate; 5g Dietary Fiber; 31mg Cholesterol; 368mg Sodium. Exchanges: 2 Lean Meat; 2 1/2 Vegetable; 1/2 Fat.

STRATA FROM NAN

A flavorful egg and cheese dish- perfect for brunch.
Servings: 2

1 slice bread, ripped in pieces
1/2 cup Jarlsberg cheese, grated
2 eggs
2 egg whites
1 cup nonfat milk
1/2 teaspoon Dijon mustard
salt and pepper, to taste

1. Preheat oven to 350.

2. Place broken pieces of bread in the bottom of a small baking dish, or two individual baking dishes.

3. Combine the remainder of ingredients in a food processor or blender. Process for about 20 seconds until well mixed.

4. Pour egg mixture over the bread.

5. Bake at 350 for 25-30 minutes or until it puffs up and is lightly browned.

SERVING IDEAS: Fresh fruit is wonderful with this.

NOTE: We like to put it together the night before and bake it in the morning. You can add crab or ham if you like. Another recipe from Nan Krumpschmidt! She is a good cook who likes to feed her family healthfully and fast. Her kids are great Cross Country runners!

Per Serving (excluding unknown items): 261 Calories; 13g Fat (46.4% calories from fat); 21g Protein; 13g Carbohydrate; trace Dietary Fiber; 215mg Cholesterol; 388mg Sodium. Exchanges: 1/2 Grain(Starch); 2 Lean Meat; 1/2 Non-Fat Milk; 1 1/2 Fat; 0 Other Carbohydrates.

VEGETABLE FRITTATA

Vegetables in an egg and cheese custard.
Servings: 2

1 egg
2 egg whites
1/2 cup nonfat cottage cheese
1/2 teaspoon olive oil
1 small onion, diced
1 1/2 cups vegetables (broccoli, spinach, zucchini, or whatever you have) , chopped
2 ounces lowfat cheddar cheese, grated
salt and pepper, to taste

1. Heat an electric skillet or heavy nonstick pan. The pan should be quite small for serving only two. Saute onion in olive oil until transparent.

2. Add other vegetables and cook until tender but not soft, stirring frequently.

3. Beat egg, egg whites and a splash of milk with cottage cheese. Pour over the vegetables, turn down heat to medium low and cover. Cook without stirring until egg is almost firm on top.

4. Sprinkle grated cheese over the frittata and cook covered until cheese melts. Cut in pieces and serve hot, seasoned to taste.

SERVING IDEAS: Serve with whole wheat toast and juice for breakfast; with fruit and bread for brunch; or with steamed vegetables, a baked potato, and/or green salad for dinner. A sprinkle of Parmesan cheese in place of some of the cheddar adds a lot of flavor.

NOTE: If you have a Food Processor, combine the eggs, cottage cheese and milk in it and process to blend before pouring over vegetable mixture.

Per Serving (excluding unknown items): 164 Calories; 5g Fat (29.8% calories from fat); 21g Protein; 7g Carbohydrate; 1g Dietary Fiber; 102mg Cholesterol; 407mg Sodium. Exchanges: 3 Lean Meat; 1 Vegetable; 1/2 Fat.

VEGETARIAN BURRITO

A vegetarian burrito that can be dressed up as you like.
Servings: 1

1 flour tortilla, lowfat or whole wheat
1/4 cup pinto beans, cooked , nonfat canned are best!
1 ounce lowfat cheddar cheese, grated
1 lettuce leaf, torn
1/4 tomato, diced
1 teaspoon onion, chopped
salsa, to taste

1. Put the beans and cheese into the tortilla and microwave for 1 1/2 minutes or until cheese is melted.

2. Open up the tortilla and layer vegetables and salsa inside.   Fold the tortilla over the vegetables and enjoy.

SERVING IDEAS: Light sour cream or a small amount of guacamole is good with this. You can also use left over grilled or fajita vegetables instead or lettuce and tomato. Dress this one up however you like!

NOTE: If you have more time and/or more people to serve, make a BURRITO BAR. Heat the beans and tortillas separately either in the microwave or on the stove top. Place the remainder of the ingredients in serving dishes and let people assemble their own burritos. You can do the same with tacos or tostadas ... just use corn tortilla shells.

Per Serving (excluding unknown items): 292 Calories; 7g Fat (22.5% calories from fat); 14g Protein; 42g Carbohydrate; 3g Dietary Fiber; 6mg Cholesterol; 521mg Sodium. Exchanges: 2 1/2 Grain(Starch); 1 Lean Meat; 1/2 Vegetable; 1 Fat.

VEGETARIAN LASAGNA

This is delicious and just about as easy as lasagna can get.
Servings: 4

8 oven-ready lasagne noodles
2 cups nonfat ricotta cheese
2 cups marinara sauce (your favorite)
2 cups baby spinach leaves
2 zucchini, sliced thin
1 cup mushrooms, sliced thin
2 tablespoons Parmesan cheese

1. Preheat oven to 450.

2. Place washed spinach in a glass bowl, cover and microwave for a minute to just wilt the leaves.

3. Cut up zucchini, mushroom and any other vegetables that you want to use in thin slices.

4. Spread 1/4 cup marinara sauce over the bottom of an 8x8 pan. Layer noodles, vegetables, ricotta cheese and marinara until all ingredients are gone. The noodles should be next to sauce and a layer of ricotta cheese should be the last added. Otherwise, you can layer in any order you like.

5. Sprinkle parmesan cheese over the top of the lasagna. Cover with foil.

6. Bake at 450 for 30 minutes. Remove the cover and bake for another 10 minutes until lightly browned. Let sit for about 10 minutes before serving.

SERVING IDEAS: A lightly dressed green salad makes a nice accompaniment. Parmesan Toast is also good with this.

NOTE: Use any of your favorite vegetables with this. Thinly sliced eggplant and bell pepper are also very good. Thanks to Julie Williams, Manager of The Oaks Corporate Office for ideas leading to this recipe.

Per Serving (excluding unknown items): 263 Calories; 2g Fat (5.7% calories from fat); 26g Protein; 37g Carbohydrate; 3g Dietary Fiber; 22mg Cholesterol; 302mg Sodium. Exchanges: 2 Grain(Starch); 2 1/2 Lean Meat; 1 Vegetable; 0 Fat; 0 Other Carbohydrates.

YELLOW RICE

A flavorful combination of rice, vegetables, raisins and curry.
Servings: 4

2 teaspoons olive oil
1 medium onion, chopped
1 cup red bell pepper, chopped
1 cup carrots, cut
3/4 cup Basmati rice
1 teaspoon curry powder, or to taste
1 teaspoon soy sauce
1 dash Tabasco sauce
1/4 cup raisins
1/4 teaspoon cinnamon
2 cups water

1. Heat olive oil in skillet- electric skillet works well.

2. Add veggies and stir fry until onion is golden.

3. Add rice and stir briefly.

4. Add curry, raisins, cinnamon, soy sauce and Tabasco to taste.

5. Add water, bring to boil and then simmer until done- about an hour. Taste for seasonings.

SERVING IDEAS: Serve with Apple Chutney and fruit salad. This is also good with Bombay Breast of Chicken. Freeze the left overs!

NOTE: This rice recipe, Dr. Oren's favorite, works with a variety of vegetables, but the red bell pepper looks most appealing. Apple Chutney is easy and quick to make- I like to keep it on hand for all curry dishes. You'll find the recipe in this book.

Per Serving (excluding unknown items): 200 Calories; 3g Fat (14.4% calories from fat); 4g Protein; 40g Carbohydrate; 3g Dietary Fiber; 0mg Cholesterol; 127mg Sodium. Exchanges: 1 1/2 Grain(Starch); 1 1/2 Vegetable; 1/2 Fruit; 1/2 Fat.

Delicious Desserts

There is no reason why desserts cannot build health. Fruit is another of God's most wonderful gifts to mankind. They are among the best sources of antioxidants, vitamins, minerals and fiber.

A perfectly ripened piece of fruit can be a fine dessert or mini-meal by itself. However, since many people feel that dessert should be served in a bowl with a spoon, we have included several fruit-based desserts that are enhanced with a topping and are sure to please.

There is also a simple and unique cookie recipe in this section, and the Gingerbread Delight should not be missed!

ALMOND ROSE WATER COOKIES

A hard almond cookie with the subtle taste of rose water.
Servings: 30

1 cup blanched almonds
1 cup sugar
1 cup all-purpose flour
2 teaspoons rose water
3 egg whites
vegetable cooking spray

1. Preheat oven to 325.

2. Place almonds in food processor and process until finely ground.

3. Add sugar and flour. Process until well mixed.

4. Add rose water and egg whites. Process until well blended. Dough will be very sticky.

5. Lightly coat cookie sheets with cooking spray.

6. Drop dough by teaspoonfuls on the cookie sheet.

7. Bake at 325 for 30 minutes or until lightly browned and crisp.

8. Cool on wire racks.

NOTE: This is similar to a cookie that my great aunt used to make for Christmas. It is easy and wonderful. These spread a lot while cooking and get hard when they cool like biscotti. We sometimes make 30 cookies and cut them in half while they are still warm. This creates a lovely little 35 calorie cookie.

Per Serving (excluding unknown items): 71 Calories; 3g Fat (31.6% calories from fat); 2g Protein; 11g Carbohydrate; trace Dietary Fiber; 0mg Cholesterol; 6mg Sodium. Exchanges: 1/2 Grain(Starch); 0 Lean Meat; 1/2 Fat; 1/2 Other Carbohydrates.

APPLE CREAM

A light mixture of whipped cream and apple sauce!
Servings: 8

1/2 cup light whipping cream
1/2 cup applesauce, unsweetened

1. Whip the cream to soft peaks with an electric mixer.

2. Fold in applesauce with a large spoon.

3. Taste for sweetness and mix in a little honey if needed.

SERVING IDEAS: Serve on top of Pumpkin Pie, Ginger Bread Delight, Baked Bananas, fruit or with broken cookies mixed in.

TRY using 3/4 cup applesauce and 1/4 cup lowfat sour cream. This drops the calories to 19 per serving.

OR TRY using 1/2 cup Cool Whip Lite® with 1/2 cup applesauce. This has only 17 calories and 1g fat per serving and tastes wonderful. Both of these alternatives take only seconds to put together- you don't even have to whip the cream!

NOTE: This recipe was introduced to us by Teddy Wolterbeek, granddaughter Rosie's "Grandmother in law". She is a wonderful role model who lives on a vineyard with her husband Al, folk dances and throws dancing parties in the barn. It is a fantastic way to reduce the calories of whipped cream.

Serving= 2 tablespoons

Per Serving (excluding unknown items): 50 Calories; 5g Fat (80.5% calories from fat); trace Protein; 2g Carbohydrate; trace Dietary Fiber; 17mg Cholesterol; 5mg Sodium.
Exchanges: 0 Fruit; 1 Fat.

BAKED BANANAS

A rich tasting banana dessert that is easy to make.
Servings: 2

1 banana, ripe
1 tablespoon maple syrup, or brown sugar
1/2 small lemon, juiced
1/2 tablespoon Butter Buds®
1/4 teaspoon rum extract

1. Preheat oven to 450.

2. Peel the banana and slice it lengthwise in half.

3. Place the halves in a small baking dish in one layer.

4. Sprinkle banana with maple syrup, lemon juice and Butter Buds®. Drizzle rum extract on top.

5. Bake until the banana is soft and the topping is bubbly- about 10 minutes. Serve hot.

SERVING IDEAS: Serve on individual plates, topped with a scoop of vanilla frozen yogurt, light ice cream or Apple Cream.

NOTE: We were amazed at how rich and delicious this tastes. Better yet, the calories are low and it's good for you! We cook it in individual dishes and serve in the same dishes ... cuts down on dishwashing and keeps the Baked Bananas hot.

Per Serving (excluding unknown items): 90 Calories; trace Fat (3.1% calories from fat); 1g Protein; 23g Carbohydrate; 2g Dietary Fiber; 0mg Cholesterol; 54mg Sodium. Exchanges: 1 Fruit; 1/2 Other Carbohydrates.

BERRIES AND CREAM

A simple, healthful, really delicious dessert!
Servings: 1

1/2 cup frozen mixed berries, or your favorite berry
2 tablespoons Cool Whip Lite®, or Apple Cream

1. In a custard cup or small bowl, microwave frozen berries for about 45 seconds or until mostly thawed.

2. Top with whipped topping and enjoy.

SERVING IDEAS: Try topping berries with vanilla nonfat yogurt for a more nutritious alternative to whipped toppings. Serve in a stemmed glass for a more elegant dessert.

NOTE: We like to keep mixed berries in our freezer for this simple dessert. If you have fresh berries, this is even more delicious and healthful. Choosing fruit for dessert is always a health-building choice, and berries are high in antioxidants.

Also try using frozen mango chunks for MANGO CHUNKS WITH TOASTED CASHEWS: Mostly thaw the mango chunks, toss with 1 tsp. of honey and top with toasted cashews, almonds or walnuts. Serve in a stemmed glass.

Per Serving (excluding unknown items): 68 Calories; 1g Fat (16.8% calories from fat); 1g Protein; 14g Carbohydrate; 4g Dietary Fiber; 0mg Cholesterol; 7mg Sodium. Exchanges: 1 Fruit; 0 Fat; 0 Other Carbohydrates.

BERRY MERINGUE GRATIN

Berries and yogurt, topped with sweet meringue...a must try!
Servings: 2

2 cups berries
1 teaspoon honey
1/3 cup plain nonfat yogurt
2 large egg whites
1 tablespoon sugar

1. Turn on the broiler to heat.

2. In a medium bowl, combine slightly thawed berries, yogurt and 1 tsp. honey.

3. Spoon yogurt-berry mixture into 2 individual baking ramekins or dishes.

4. In a deep bowl or cup, whip egg whites with a mixer at high speed until foamy. Continue to beat and gradually add sugar until whites hold stiff peaks when beaters are lifted.

5. Swirl meringue equally over yogurt-berry mixture. Broil about 4 inches from heat until meringue is browned- about 1 minute.

6. Garnish with additional berries or mint sprigs.

NOTE: This is an elegant dessert that takes a little more time than one might spend when dining alone, but it is worth doing. If you don't have the time or inclination to whip the egg whites and brown the meringue, the yogurt-berry mixture alone is also wonderful.

Per Serving (excluding unknown items): 117 Calories; 1g Fat (4.1% calories from fat); 7g Protein; 23g Carbohydrate; 3g Dietary Fiber; 1mg Cholesterol; 85mg Sodium. Exchanges: 1/2 Lean Meat; 1/2 Fruit; 0 Non-Fat Milk; 1/2 Other Carbohydrates.

GINGER BAKED PEAR

If you like ginger, you'll love this pear!
Servings: 2

1 pear, halved and pitted
1 tablespoon apple juice, frozen concentrate
1 teaspoon candied ginger root, minced

1. Put apple juice and ginger in a small microwave-safe dish.

2. Carve 3 strips from the skin of the pear.

3. Place pear cut-side-down in dish, spoon juice over pear and cover with plastic wrap.

4. Microwave on high for 5 minutes.

5. Remove pears to serving dishes.

6. Place dish with juice and ginger in microwave and cook uncovered for 2 minutes to make a syrup/glaze.

7. Spoon glaze over pears, chill and serve.

NOTE: If you don't have a thick syrup after 2 minutes, cook in 1/2 minute increments to obtain your glaze.
If you're not fond of ginger, use the same procedure with different juices.
Some people like pears with a little light wine added to the juice. This is one of our favorite desserts.

Per Serving (excluding unknown items): 70 Calories; trace Fat (4.4% calories from fat); trace Protein; 18g Carbohydrate; 2g Dietary Fiber; 2mg Cholesterol; 2mg Sodium. Exchanges: 1 Fruit; 0 Other Carbohydrates.

GINGERBREAD DELIGHT

A soft bread flavored with spices, molasses & candied ginger.
Servings: 12

2 cups whole wheat flour
1/2 cup brown sugar
1 teaspoon baking soda
1 teaspoon each ginger & cinnamon
1/2 teaspoon salt
1/2 cup molasses, blackstrap
1/2 cup nonfat plain yogurt
1/2 cup applesauce, unsweetened
1 egg
1/3 cup candied ginger root, minced fine
1/4 cup hot water

1. Preheat oven to 350.

2. Combine dry ingredients in a bowl.

3. Combine the rest of the ingredients in another bowl or large glass measuring cup.

4. Add the wet ingredients to the dry, blend and then beat with an electric mixer for 3 minutes. If the batter seems too dry, add a little more hot water.

5. Pour into a 9 x 9 pan and bake for 30 to 40 minutes at 350.

6. Cool and serve with Apple Cream (in this section). Or top with a little honey or Apple Butter.

NOTE:I developed this recipe one morning when I needed a cake to take to a friend's birthday. It was quicker than going out and shopping for a cake, and everyone liked it a lot. Share it with friends or freeze portions for later. This can also be made in a large loaf pan or 4 small loaf pans. The later makes slicing very easy.

INGREDIENT NOTE: When preparing this bread for revisions in this new edition, I used persimmon pulp from my freezer and it turned out very well.

Per Serving (excluding unknown items): 154 Calories; 1g Fat (4.4% calories from fat); 4g Protein; 35g Carbohydrate; 3g Dietary Fiber; 16mg Cholesterol; 217mg Sodium. Exchanges; 1 Grain (Starch); 0 Lean Meat; 0 Fruit; 0 Non-Fat Milk; 0 Fat; 1 Other Carbohydrates.

HONEYED FRUIT WITH YOGURT & WALNUTS

A treat from Israel.
Servings: 1

2 tablespoons nonfat yogurt
1 teaspoon honey
1/4 cup pear, cut in 1/2" cubes
2 tablespoons red grapes, halved
2 tablespoons strawberries, sliced
2 teaspoons walnuts, or pecans, chopped, toasted and cooled

1. Combine fruit in a dish and toss with honey, using more or less honey to taste.

2. Spread yogurt over fruit to cover.

3. Sprinkle yogurt with walnuts or pecans.

NOTE: Of course you will vary the fruits according to the season and your taste. This is best made immediately before serving.
Dr. Ami Oren first served this to my husband and me at a luncheon overlooking the Venice Canals. Husband Stan loved it!

Per Serving (excluding unknown items): 112 Calories; 3g Fat (24.3% calories from fat); 3g Protein; 20g Carbohydrate; 2g Dietary Fiber; 1mg Cholesterol; 23mg Sodium. Exchanges: 0 Grain(Starch); 0 Lean Meat; 1/2 Fruit; 0 Non-Fat Milk; 1/2 Fat; 1/2 Other Carbohydrates.

LEMON YOGURT SAUCE AND PINEAPPLE SUPREME

Nonfat yogurt with a touch of lemon curd.
Servings: 2

1 tablespoon Lemon Curd
1/2 cup vanilla nonfat yogurt

Combine and mix with a fork or small wisk.

SERVING IDEAS: Serve as a dip for fruit for an hors d'oeuvre or dessert. This would also be a good topping for the Ginger Bread Delight or Carrot Bread in this book.

LEMON PINEAPPLE SUPREME: Toss lemon yogurt sauce with pineapple cubes right before serving. Serve in stemmed glasses garnished with a flower or mint leaves for an elegant dessert. People are always amazed and delighted with the flavor of this dish.

Per Serving (excluding unknown items): 32 Calories; 0g Fat (0.0% calories from fat); 3g Protein; 4g Carbohydrate; 0g Dietary Fiber; 1mg Cholesterol; 47mg Sodium. Exchanges: .

OLD FASHIONED CORNSTARCH PUDDING

A simple pudding that can be put together out of your pantry.
Servings: 2

2 tablespoons sugar
1 tablespoon cornstarch
1 cup nonfat milk
1/2 teaspoon vanilla
pinch salt

1. Combine sugar and cornstarch in a 2-cup glass measuring cup.

2. Stir in milk, whisking until smooth.

3. Microwave uncovered on high for 2 minutes, whisk smooth and repeat twice (6 minutes total).

4. Divide into serving dishes and chill.

SERVING IDEAS: Top with a sprinkle of nutmeg. Garnish with a sliver of fruit and a sprig of mint for more elegant presentation.

NOTE: If you prefer chocolate pudding, add 2 ounces of coursely chopped dark chocolate to the milk before microwaving. This more than doubles the calories. For a thicker pudding, use Evaporated Skim Milk.

Per Serving (excluding unknown items): 110 Calories; trace Fat (1.8% calories from fat); 4g Protein; 22g Carbohydrate; trace Dietary Fiber; 2mg Cholesterol; 64mg Sodium. Exchanges: 0 Grain(Starch); 1/2 Non-Fat Milk; 1 Other Carbohydrates.

STUFFED BAKED APPLE

Better than apple pie! And quickly done in the microwave.
Servings: 2

1 apple (green cooking apples are best), halved and pitted
2 tablespoons dates, pitted and chopped
1 tablespoon walnuts, chopped
1/2 teaspoon Butter Buds®
2 teaspoons honey

1. Score the apple skin and carve out a little hollow the cut side.

2. Spread honey over the cut side of the apple and sprinkle with Butter Buds®.

3. Place the apple halves, cut-side-down, in a microwave-safe baking dish. Cover with plastic wrap.

4. Microwave on high for 3 minutes.

5. Combine dates and walnuts.

6. Turn apples cut-side-up, and place date mixture in hollow of apple. Spoon juices over apples.

7. Microwave 1 minute uncovered and place apples on serving dishes.

8. Spoon remaining juice over the apples to glaze.

SERVING IDEAS: Serve warm or chilled. The Apple Cream in this book is a nice topping, but a little ice cream, yogurt or sour cream is good also. We actually prefer it plain.

NOTE: Scoring the apple skin makes this easier to eat and the flavor is better absorbed. Be sure to cut right up to the edges of the skin.

Per Serving (excluding unknown items): 118 Calories; 2g Fat (17.3% calories from fat); 1g Protein; 25g Carbohydrate; 3g Dietary Fiber; 0mg Cholesterol; 18mg Sodium. Exchanges: 0 Grain(Starch); 0 Lean Meat; 1 Fruit; 1/2 Fat; 1/2 Other Carbohydrates.

INDEX

NOTES FROM 2005

It has been four years since we published Healthy Cooking for Singles & Doubles and much has changed.

Eleanor will be 80 next year and is still food consultant at The Oaks at Ojai. She also continues to teach yoga at The Oaks and maintains an active lifestyle which includes an annual ski trip with her family. She is not planning to retire. Robin married the love of her life, Scott Detmer, and is blissfully happy. She finished graduate school and is now a Physical Therapist.

There have also been changes in nutritional and food preparation recommendations in the last four years.

1. Microwave cooking with plastic wrap has come under some scrutiny. We recommend making sure the plastic wrap you buy says "microwave safe" or that you use a glass lid or corning ware for heating.

2. Albacore tuna has been shown to contain more mercury than light tuna so we recommend using water packed light tuna.

3. We've known that hydrogenated and partially hydrogenated oils are bad for the heart and arteries. Recent studies suggest that these oils also attack brain tissue, destroying memory and decreasing thought processes. We recommend reading labels and staying clear of these oils. Clean out your cupboards!

4. High fructose corn syrup is thought to be linked to obesity. It has been shown to suppress leptin, decreasing the body's sense of fullness, and increase fats in the blood. Our recommendation is again to read labels and avoid high fructose corn syrup.

A few things that have not changed: the less food is processed, the better. The more colorful the fruits and vegetables on your plate, the more efficiently your immune system works. And the best way to good health and weight control is still regular exercise and healthful food choices.